Praise for Noah St. John

"Noah's method is one of the most significant breakthroughs in the study of success in decades. If you want to eliminate the fear of success and live the life you've imagined, you owe it to yourself to attend his programs."

— **Jack Canfield,** author of the
Chicken Soup for the Soul series

"Using humor and down-to-earth language, Noah gives you a step-by-step method to live the life you want and deserve."

— **John Gray, Ph.D.,** author of
Men Are from Mars, Women Are from Venus

"Noah St. John speaks the language we all want to understand: how to make the most of your life and career."

— **Harvey Mackay,** author of *Swim with the Sharks Without Being Eaten Alive*

"Noah St. John's work is about discovering within ourselves what we should have known all along—we are truly powerful beings with unlimited potential."

— **Stephen Covey,** author of
The 7 Habits of Highly Effective People

"You'll never get your foot off the brake and find the success you dream of until you take Noah's advice to heart!"

— **T. Harv Eker,** author of *Secrets of the Millionaire Mind*

"Noah is a brilliant guy who brings tremendous insight into this problem of embracing success he quite accurately observes in people."

— **Neale Donald Walsch,** author of the
Conversations with God series

THE **BOOK** OF
AFFORMATIONS®

ALSO BY NOAH ST. JOHN

Books

The Secret Code of Success:
7 Hidden Steps to More Wealth and Happiness

Permission to Succeed®:
Unlocking the Mystery of Success Anorexia

Audios

iAfform Audios: Done-For-You Afformations®
Audios to Help You Manifest Your Desires
While You're Busy Doing Other Things

Afformware: Do-It-Yourself Afformations® Audios
to Change Your Brain and Change Your Life

Home-Study Programs

The Afformations® System:
28 Days to a More Abundant Lifestyle

Power Habits: The New Science
for Making Success Automatic

All of the above are available at **www.NoahStJohn.com**

THE **BOOK** OF
AFFORMATIONS®

Discovering the
Missing Piece to
Abundant Health,
Wealth, Love,
and Happiness

BY NOAH ST. JOHN
FOREWORD BY JOHN ASSARAF

HAY HOUSE, INC.
Carlsbad, California • New York City
London • Sydney • Johannesburg
Vancouver • Hong Kong • New Delhi

Published and distributed in the United States by: Hay House, Inc.:
www.hayhouse.com® • *Published and distributed in Australia by:*
Hay House Australia Pty. Ltd.: www.hayhouse.com.au • *Published
and distributed in the United Kingdom by:* Hay House UK, Ltd.:
www.hayhouse.co.uk • *Published and distributed in the Republic
of South Africa by:* Hay House SA (Pty), Ltd.: www.hayhouse.co.za
Distributed in Canada by: Raincoast: www.raincoast.com • *Published in India by:* Hay House Publishers India: www.hayhouse.co.in

Indexer: Jay Kreider
Cover design: Amy Rose Grigoriou
Interior design: Riann Bender

Library of Congress Cataloging-in-Publication Data

St. John, Noah.
The book of afformations : discovering the missing piece to abundant health, wealth, love, and happiness / by Noah St. John ; foreword
by John Assaraf. -- 1st edition.
    pages cm
Includes index.
ISBN 978-1-4019-4304-2 (tradepaper : alk. paper) 1. Affirmations.
2. Success. I. Title.
BF697.5.S47S72 2013
158--dc23
                                      2013012239

Hardcover ISBN: 978-1-4019-4414-8

16 15 14 13   4 3 2 1
1st Hay House edition, August 2013

This is the fourth edition of this book. Previous editions copyrighted
in 2001, 2004, and 2008 and published by Success Clinic International, LLC.

Printed in the United States of America

*This book is dedicated to Babette:
my wife, best friend, and
the best Loving Mirror I've ever had.*

*And to Afformers everywhere:
Those who ask better questions
to make this world a better place
for all of God's creatures.*

Support your local library, teacher, or school—
10 percent of all author royalties
are donated to educational nonprofits,
including Donorschoose.org

CONTENTS

FOREWORD

When I was in my early 20s, my first serious mentor told me that my words become my thoughts, my thoughts become my emotions, and my emotions will determine what I follow and do.

Up until then, I hadn't paid much attention to the inner dialogue going on in my head. In essence, I was ignorant of the fact that all success or failure begins with a person's self-talk and self-thought.

But once I grasped the full potential of the power that existed within my own mind, I immediately began practicing having a positive mental attitude. Whenever I caught myself thinking or talking negatively to myself or to one of my friends, I'd quickly correct myself and rephrase it into a positive message.

Every day I'd repeat positive affirmations and apply visualization techniques to train my brain to be positive and clear of the mental crap I used to have.

At the time, I really wasn't sure about the effects of all the positive material I was feeding my mind, but I do remember that it sure felt better than being negative and feeling insecure and uncertain of my future! Yet almost immediately, my success started to accelerate . . . and it hasn't stopped for the past 30 years.

When I read Noah St. John's brand-new fourth edition of *The Book of Afformations*, I instantly loved how he's taken the very best of today's new knowledge about the brain and created a system that really forces you to think about why and how you can achieve any of the goals you choose—instead of listening to the doubts, fears, and uncertainties that may be holding you back from all the success you desire.

If affirmations are what worked in the past, Afformations are what work now.

Achieving success doesn't have to be hard. Follow the lessons in this book, and discover how easy it can be for you to make a significant leap forward in your health, wealth, relationships, business, and any other area in your life.

> If affirmations are what worked in the past, Afformations are what work now.

The stories in this book will warm your heart and make you realize that you have it within you to succeed beyond your wildest dreams.

But let me warn you: this isn't a book to be read in one sitting. I'll bet you'll read a few pages and then pause and really *think* about how to apply the genius content you've just read. Then you'll do it over and over again throughout this amazing book.

I'm super excited for you because I deeply know that the power of applying Noah's method can literally transform your life—and help you create the masterpiece you truly want and are capable of achieving!

To your ongoing success,
John Assaraf,
New York Times best-selling author and CEO, **Praxisnow.com**

• ● •

HOW THIS BOOK WAS WRITTEN—AND WHY

"The starting point is a question."

— ALBERTO MANGUEL

Did you ever notice how the best ideas come to you in the shower?

It happens all the time. You're minding your own business, holding the shampoo bottle, when suddenly it hits you.

The idea that would change everything.

The solution to the problem you've been facing.

The answer to the question you've been asking.

And it was right in front of you all along. . . .

• • •

April 24, 1997. A crisp spring morning in New England. I'm living in a dorm room at the small liberal arts college where I'm majoring in religious studies. The dorm room itself is so big that when I stand in the middle of the room, I can touch the walls on either side.

At this point in my life, I'm 30 years old, divorced, and have less than $800 to my name. I also have no idea what I'm going to do with the rest of my life.

On the night before *The Shower That Changed Everything,* I'm sitting in my tiny room, staring at the concrete walls, when three thoughts occur to me. The first thought is that something is very wrong with my life; that much is obvious. The second thought, which bothers me even more than the first, is that I have no idea how to fix my life; that one definitely bugs me. And the third thought, which annoys me even more than the first two, is that if anyone should be successful, it should be me; and since I'm anything *but* successful, I feel like a total failure.

> That night, I realize that something is very wrong with my life.

Let me explain.

I grew up in a poor family in a rich neighborhood. Although we lived in one of the wealthiest communities in New England, my family was dirt poor. I mean that literally: we lived at the bottom of a dirt road in an unfinished house. One day when I was about nine years old, I asked my mother, "Mom, how come you and Dad are always fighting about money? And how come we always have to eat macaroni and cheese?"

My mother replied that they constantly fought about money because there was not enough coming in, and she was afraid they wouldn't be able to pay the bills and keep food on the table. When she said that, I was very confused, because I saw both my father and mother working all the time. Weeks would go by and we'd hardly see my father, because he'd be working 70 to 80 hours a week or more. And my mother worked part-time jobs, too. So I asked her the next logical question:

"Why isn't there enough money coming in?"

I don't think my mother really knew how to answer that question, so she took out the family checkbook and showed me how much money was coming in and going out every month. Sure enough, there was more *month* left at the end of the *money.*

At that moment, I made two decisions that would profoundly affect the rest of my life. First, I decided that I wouldn't need anything from my parents and that I'd become self-sufficient as quickly as possible. Now, I'm sure that was not my mother's intention; nevertheless, at that moment I decided to not ask my parents for things, because I didn't want to be a burden to them.

The second decision I made was that I would make something of my life, even though I had no idea what that meant, let alone how to do it. But I decided that I didn't want to live a life of lack and fear and poverty. That was all I knew, all I had ever known; but I decided then and there that it wasn't the life I wanted.

You've heard of the book *Rich Dad, Poor Dad?* Well, I only had a poor dad. My father, even though he worked hard all his life, couldn't teach me how to be successful. Since I didn't know who else to ask, I decided to use the library. I began devouring the classics of self-help literature: Dale Carnegie, Napoleon Hill, Wayne Dyer,

Stephen Covey, and more. I spent most of my childhood in the library, because books were a way for me to escape from that life of poverty, lack, and fear.

I also made sure to work hard and apply myself in school, because I naturally assumed that the best way to succeed in life was to get good grades (since that's what everyone told us). I got straight A's, skipped eighth grade, graduated at the top of my class, and got full scholarships to college. By the time I graduated from high school, my parents, teachers, and friends were telling me that I was going to be a big success.

Yet, there I sat in my pocket-sized dorm room all those years later, with nothing to show for all my hard work but a series of missed opportunities, failed relationships, and less than $800 in the bank.

For as long as I could remember, I'd had this inescapable, gnawing feeling that there was something missing—some vital piece of information I'd overlooked, some secret key that would unlock the vault to success. But the harder I looked, the more the answer seemed to elude me.

That was the day The Shower happened.

● ● ●

The night before The Shower That Changed Everything, something else happens that's important to our story. As I'm sitting in my miniature dorm room thinking about how my life pretty much sucks, I look around the room and see something. In fact, I see lots and lots of somethings.

I realize that the walls of my dorm room are covered with pieces of yellow legal paper on which I'd written dozens of positive statements, such as: *I am happy, I am wealthy,* and *I am good enough.*

Why had I posted all these positive statements all over my dorm room? Because that's what all those self-help books I'd been reading for so many years had said to do!

That night, I finally admit something that I'd never wanted to admit before—that even though I'd spent most of my life trying to convince myself of the truth of these positive statements, I never really believed them. As much as I *wanted* to believe that I was happy, wealthy, and good enough, I didn't believe any of those things. In fact, the harder I tried to believe those positive things about my life, the more the cold, hard facts stared back at me and seemed to say, *"Yeah, right!"*

I turn out the light and go to bed feeling depressed, defeated, and discouraged.

The next day, I get up and get in the shower, just like any other morning. Except on this particular morning, my mind is still racing from the night before. Questions start bouncing around my brain—questions that are simple, yet profound. If you could have heard what was going on in my head at that exact moment, it would have sounded like this:

If I've been saying these positive statements to myself for so many years, how come I still don't believe them?

And if I <u>don't</u> believe these positive statements after repeating them over and over again for so long, what's it going to take for me to finally believe something good about myself?

There's got to be an easier way to change my life. But what is it?

That's when it hit me. (No, not the soap.)

I realize that what I'm doing at that very moment is asking and searching for answers to questions. In that instant, I realize that *human thought itself is the process of asking and searching for answers to questions.*

Suddenly, a question forms in my mind—a simple question that changes everything:

> *If human thought is the process of asking and searching for answers to <u>questions,</u> why are we going around making statements that we don't believe?*

In a flash of insight, I finally understand why I never believed all those positive statements I'd been repeating over and over all those years. It all came down to one simple thing. Of course! It was so obvious now that I saw it. I immediately recognize that it doesn't matter how long or how often I repeat these positive statements to myself; if I don't fix this one single thing, all of my hard work will be for naught.

At that moment, I knew that if we start to ask ourselves the right questions, it would change everything.

Then something else occurs to me. I realize there are *millions* of people just like me—people who are trying really hard to change their lives, people who are "following the rules" just like we were told, but who still haven't manifested the abundant lifestyle they really want—because they didn't believe the positive statements they'd been saying to themselves, either.

At that moment, I had the realization that if we were to start to *ask ourselves the right questions* and *stop asking the wrong questions,* it would literally change everything.

And for the first time, I know in the depths of my soul what I'm here on Earth to do.

That's why, on the morning of April 24, 1997, I got out of the shower . . . and realized that everything was about to change.

● ● ●

After my epiphany in The Shower That Changed Everything, I immediately sat down at my computer and typed out a question that consisted of four simple words. As I stared at the words glowing on my computer screen, I had another thought: *If I accept the truth of this question—and start acting as if it were true—then my life would have to change.*

Then I wrote another question, as simple as the first one. Then another. Then another. The questions kept coming. I kept writing. For the first time in my life, everything finally made sense.

After I'd typed several pages of questions, I stopped and stared at my monitor again. The words I'd just written were different from every positive statement I'd ever read or heard or written or spoken in my entire life. I knew this, because in all my years of research and study, I'd never seen anyone articulate thoughts in this way.

Then I had another thought: *What am I supposed to do now?*

This is so cool! I thought. *I can't believe no one's ever thought of this before!* Then I had another thought, one that stopped me in my tracks: *What am I supposed to do now?*

But I didn't yet have an answer to that question. That's why, after The Shower That Changed Everything, even though I knew my life was about to change, I still didn't know how to change it. I went about the business of being a broke 30-year-old religious studies major—and tucked my discovery away, until I could figure out what to do with it.

Six months later, on October 20, 1997, I had the second epiphany that changed my life, when I realized the existence of a condition I named *success anorexia,* which causes people to hold themselves back from the level of success they're capable of. That discovery led to the publication of my first book, *Permission to Succeed®,* and eventually my other books, seminars, workshops, and mastermind programs, where I teach people how to live a more abundant lifestyle and stop driving down the road of life with one foot on the brake.

And in all of my seminars, keynote speeches, products, and programs, I kept teaching people about my discovery that happened in The Shower That Changed Everything—and the simple four-step method I invented to change your questions, change your results, and change your life. (I'll teach you these four steps in Part II of this book.)

As the years went on, and as I kept sharing my method through books, TV interviews, live workshops, and online events, something wonderful began to happen: people around the world started sending me cards, letters, and e-mails; sharing their stories on social media; and telling me in our seminars and mastermind groups about the amazing results they were getting by using my simple method—results like:

- Getting promotions after feeling completely stuck in their careers
- Growing their business after sales had been stagnant for years
- Adding five, six, seven, and yes, even *eight figures* to their income
- Finally losing weight after they'd tried every diet and exercise program on the market
- Finding the man or woman of their dreams after giving up on relationships
- Starting the home-based business they'd been dreaming of
- Completing their book that had languished unfinished for years
- Healing family relationships that had been broken
- Quitting smoking after they'd tried everything else
- Sleeping better after pills and medications hadn't helped
- Schoolchildren improving their grades almost overnight
- Winning golf tournaments and other sporting events for the first time . . . and many, many, many more.

Then those people began to tell their friends, and those friends told *their* friends . . . and so on and so on . . . and that's how *The Afformations Revolution* began.

And it all started with a simple question that I asked in the shower.

• • •

This book was written for you, if you . . .

- . . . want to live a *happier, healthier, wealthier life*

- . . . want to be *free from money worries*

- . . . are struggling to *overcome procrastination, self-doubt, overeating, smoking, or any other bad habit*

- . . . want to *quickly and easily boost your health and your self-confidence*

- . . . want *better financial results* in your career or business

- . . . are seeking to *find the balance* between your faith, your family, and your career

- . . . are looking for *more purpose or passion* at work

- . . . want to *attract the man or woman you've been waiting for*

- . . . want to *get out of overwhelm and get unstuck now*

- . . . are looking for *a faster, easier, less stressful way to live a more abundant lifestyle*

This book holds the answers to questions you've had for years—and provides answers to the ones you didn't even know you had.

Enjoy it from beginning to end. Share the method with your friends, family members, and co-workers.

And prepare to be amazed as the miracle of your new, abundant lifestyle unfolds before you.

I believe in you!

Noah

Noah St. John
Inventor of Afformations®
Founder of **SuccessClinic.com**

•　●　•

TOP 10 (+1) WAYS TO GET THE MOST FROM THIS BOOK

*"The question is not what you look at,
but what you see."*

— HENRY DAVID THOREAU

1. Read through the entire book.

I know you're busy. That's why I've written this book in an easy-to-digest, step-by-step format. Think of it as a foundational course on how to unlock your brain's natural ability to manifest your desires faster, easier, and with far less effort.

I've also designed *The Book of Afformations* so you can take it with you wherever you go and refer to it throughout the day (see #10 that follows). That makes this book the perfect companion for today's busy person!

2. Set the book down and wonder.

After you've read this book through the first time, put it down for a while. Take a walk. Look at the sky. Breathe the air. Let new ideas come to you.

As new thoughts and creative ideas come, start an Afformations Journal so you can capture them in writing and then act on them. Remember the ancient proverb: "The palest ink is stronger than the sharpest memory."

3. Highlight the passages that have special meaning to you.

When certain ideas, phrases, or questions in this book bring up strong feelings in you, highlight or underline those passages so you can refer to them later. There are also places in this book where I ask you to do certain exercises. Make sure you follow the instructions so you get the most out of them.

I've had the privilege of teaching this method to tens of thousands of people in over 50 countries, so I've taken all the guesswork out of the process for you. I've also identified the shortcuts to help you reach your goals faster—as well as the hazards to avoid!

In addition, be sure to write the date next to the passages you highlight, so each time you revisit this book in the future, you'll see just how far you've come. This will also be a powerful reminder to your subconscious mind of the progress you've made, which in turn will boost your confidence to keep taking action toward your goals.

4. Use the questions in this book to guide you, but don't feel limited by them.

Throughout this book, I'll give you hundreds of examples of empowering questions you can use to change your life. But since there is an infinite number of empowering questions you can ask, don't feel limited by the ones I give you here. Instead, use them as jumping-off points for your own Afformations that suit your personal goals and desires.

As I've mentioned, in Part II you'll learn my simple four-step method to change your life using empowering Afformations. Right now, the questions you're asking are creating your life. But I'll show you how to finally harness that incredible power to work in your favor!

5. Share this method with your friends at least twice in the next 48 hours.

Research suggests that when you share this method at least twice in the next 48 hours—once with your loved ones and once with your co-workers and business colleagues—it will help you more fully absorb and use it in your own life.

You'll get more out of this method when you tell your friends about it.

In addition, sharing this method with your friends and colleagues will make it that much harder to go back to the old, disempowering way of thinking.

As you begin this process right now, think of specific people in your life—your family members, friends, and work associates—with whom you'd like to share this method. Then, share it with them—through social media or just by talking to them—in the next 48 hours and while it's still fresh in your mind!

6. Allow this method to be as simple as it is.

People at my seminars and mastermind groups sometimes feel a little embarrassed by how simple The Afformations Method is—because once you start using Afformations properly, it can often feel like you're not working at all!

The fact is, since most of us are used to the idea of "working hard" to get what we want, it can feel counter-intuitive to *not* work hard to get what we want. That's why the hardest work can often be to simply *allow things to happen.*

It's true: we often need to work hard to get what we want in life. For example, if you want to build a new house, it will not just magically appear all by itself. A house must be built using applied knowledge and disciplined action. However, consider that many of the rarest and most precious things in life—love, peace, serenity, joy, and happiness, for example—occur not because we "work hard" at them but because we *allow* them to happen. Let this method be that simple for you.

7. Remember the difference between *simple* and *easy.*

This may sound like a contradiction (but it isn't), re-member that there is a very important distinction be-tween *simple* and *easy. Simple* means something that is not complicated, complex, or difficult to understand. *Easy* means something that takes little to no effort to accomplish. What is simple is not always easy. In fact, one of the biggest problems in our industry is that people often confuse *simple* and *easy.*

For example, baking a cake is both simple and easy. There is a simple recipe to follow to produce the result you want. When you follow the recipe, you have a high likelihood of success. However, reaching a significant personal goal—such as losing weight, climbing a mountain, or writing a book—may be simple in theory, but will take disciplined effort and concerted action to accomplish. Significant personal achievements like this, therefore, should not really be considered "easy."

> There's a big difference between *simple* and *easy.*

As human beings, it's natural to feel great when we have quick success with something. This is what's often referred to as "beginner's luck." However, the true test is when we run into challenges that test our resolve; do we quit, or do we keep going?

Thousands of my clients from around the world have shared with me their personal stories of how using Afformations has changed their lives—both immediately and for the long term. But just because The Afformations Method is both stunningly simple and astonishingly effective doesn't mean that you won't have to *do something different* to get the results you want.

> When you run into challenges, will you quit or keep going?

Let's be clear: If you want to get results, you will have to *do something.* You will have to *take action.* I'm not one of those teachers who says, "Just think about money and the money will start pouring in!" Ah, no—it won't. (Gosh darn it!)

If you want to get different results in your life, you'll have to let go of certain things you've been thinking, saying, and doing that no longer serve you. And you must be willing to truthfully examine your assumptions about life and change your behavior accordingly.

If, however, you are willing to follow the four steps of The Afformations Method—and don't give up when you run into challenges or setbacks—you will be amazed by the results, just like so many people around the world who've used it.

8. Do the exercises.

If you want to lose weight and get in shape, you can't do it by reading a book. If you want to build a house, it won't get built by you staring at the blueprints and not taking action. You must follow the instructions and *take action.*

Yes, it takes time, practice, and effort. But if you stick with it, the result will be a healthier body, new house, or whatever it is you're trying to accomplish—coupled with a wonderful sense of satisfaction for a job well done.

> You can't lose weight by reading a book about how to do it. You must also *take action.*

You'll find that The Afformations Method works in the same way. The benefits you will experience will far outweigh the time and effort you invest. That's why I highly recommend that you start an Afformations Journal to do the activities I suggest as you read this book and follow the instructions I outline here.

9. Share your experiences with me.

I love to hear Afformations success stories! No matter who you are or where you're from, you can share your story at the official Afformations fan page: **www.Afformation Nation.com**.

There you'll see photos, videos, and success stories posted by people from around the world who have used Afformations to change their lives. You'll feel inspired reading about other people's experiences and how they overcame life's challenges using this method. And you'll also have the chance to meet other Afformers (an Afformer is a person who uses Afformations; a member of The Afformations Revolution; or someone who shares The Afformations Method with friends, family, and co-workers) around the world—and it's 100 percent free!

My amazing support staff and I are also here to help you any time you have questions, want support, or would like to go to the next level with your education and create a more abundant lifestyle for yourself and your family. Visit our main websites:

- **NoahStJohn.com**: For home-study programs, videos, books, personal coaching, mastermind groups, and live events

- **Afformations.com**: Free video training on Afformations

- **iAfform.com**: Done-for-you Afformations audio recordings to help you manifest your desires while you're busy doing other things

10. Every morning for the next 40 days, open this book and choose an empowering Afformation for that day.

My clients often tell me that they start their day by opening their *Book of Afformations* in the morning and letting their eyes fall on a "random" Afformation. They often tell me it's the exact one they needed for inspiration that day!

> Every morning, open this book and choose an Afformation for the day.

Follow this practice for the next 40 days. Then do it again for the next 40. (With a name like Noah, you get used to working in 40-day intervals.)

You'll be amazed at how such a simple practice can make such a big difference in your life.

11. Finally, remember your two most important jobs on Earth.

1. To be a blessing to others.
2. To give yourself *permission to succeed.*

As you bless others, let yourself be blessed. As you give yourself *permission to succeed,* you give others that same permission.

As you use Afformations, I encourage you to let more abundance manifest in your life—faster and easier than you ever thought possible.

> As you use Afformations, you'll let abundance manifest in your life—faster and easier than you ever thought possible.

Share the gift of *you* with others, and watch your life and the lives of those around you change for the better. That's how, working together, we can change the world.

P.S. I hope to see *your* success story in one of my up-coming Afformations books!

• ● •

PART I

WHAT ARE AFFORMATIONS?

CHAPTER 1

WHAT'S MISSING IN YOUR LIFE?

*"Every sentence I utter must be understood
not as an affirmation, but as a question."*

— NIELS BOHR

Would you like to change your life? Would you like to have . . .

- . . . more control over your choices every day?

- . . . more free time to spend with your family?

- . . . a more fulfilling career?

- . . . more money to enjoy the good things in life?

- . . . more vibrant health?

- . . . deep, blissful sleep?

- . . . lower stress?

- . . . happier relationships?
- . . . greater satisfaction at work?
- . . . a better love life?
- . . . a more abundant lifestyle?

Of course you would. That's why you're reading this book!

I'm sure this isn't the first book of this type you've read. In fact, you've probably tried many things to achieve results like the ones I just listed. Let me ask you a question:

What have you tried to do to change your life?

If you're like the thousands of men and women I've spoken to at my seminars or coached in our mastermind groups, you've probably tried:

- Reading self-help books
- Buying personal-growth programs
- Attending conferences and seminars
- Working on your communication or relationship skills
- Starting a new diet or exercise program
- Joining a gym
- Writing out your goals
- Doing vision boards
- Using affirmations or positive statements

Hey, wait a minute! What's that last one?

If you've ever read a self-help book or tried anything in the personal-growth industry, it's very likely that you've tried using affirmations or positive statements to change your life. Studies show that millions of people have been writing, speaking, and listening to positive statements for years—perhaps even decades. So let's begin at the beginning. . . .

Question: Why have so many of us spent so much time saying, writing, and listening to positive statements?

Answer: Because that's what we were told to do.

> We've used positive statements for years, because that's what we were told to do.

Highly successful people over the years have told you, me, and millions of others that if we wanted to change our lives, we should use positive statements. And who were the individuals telling us to follow this method? Those who I call "traditional success teachers."

These highly successful people told us in books, seminars, lectures, and movies— pretty much everywhere we looked—that there was another traditional success teacher telling us that we should use positive statements if we wanted to change our lives. So, of course we tried it.

Which brings us to the next question. . . .

Question (and this is really important): Do positive statements actually work to change our lives?

Answer: Of course they do. There's no doubt that positive statements or affirmations have helped millions of people achieve their personal and professional goals.

But there's just one teeny little problem. . . .

Question: How come I've tried using affirmations and didn't get what I wanted?

Answer: Because there was something missing.

What Your Mind Can Do

The human mind is an incredibly miraculous thing. For example, it created the computer I'm typing these words on right now. It is a human mind—your mind—that is reading these words and processing their meaning in a split second.

If you are reading these words in a building right now (for instance, your home, your office, the library, and so on), the human mind created that. If you're reading this book in a car, truck, minivan, or commuter train, the human mind created that, too. (I just hope you're not reading while driving!) Nevertheless, if you're in a building or vehicle right now, the human mind conceived it, and lots of human minds (and bodies) worked together to build it.

Consider that the human mind also created the fields of science, religion, philosophy, mathematics, history, and every work of art that has ever existed. Here are just a few of the things your miraculous mind can do:

Analyze, brainstorm, create, dream, engineer, form, generate, have a hunch, imagine, judge, know, learn, meditate, originate, plan, rationalize, speculate, think, understand, visualize, and *wonder.*

Isn't that amazing? And you can do all of that before breakfast!

We often forget what a miracle our own mind is. We often think of ourselves as static, fixed, unchanging beings: *I am what I am, and that's that.* But consider this for a moment: have you *always* been the person you are right now? Are you the same person today as when you . . .

- • . . . took your first step?
- • . . . first rode a bike?
- • . . . attended your first day of school?
- • . . . opened your first bank account?
- • . . . learned how to drive?
- • . . . went on your first date?
- • . . . got married?
- • . . . had your first child?

All of these stages of life have one thing in common—each one meant *change*. You underwent *change* when you went from crawling to walking . . . from being dependent to being independent . . . from single to married . . . from working at a job to owning your own business.

Life, at its essence, is change. In fact, every day of your life means change, because every day you are a different person from the day before.

> Life, at its essence, is change.

Now, here's where things get *really* interesting. . . .

What the Traditional Success Teachers Taught You

What is an *affirmation?* Simply put, it's a statement of something you want to be true in your life.

Your thoughts are like seeds. You plant these *thought-seeds* every minute of every hour of every day of your life, whether you're aware of it or not. As you think about anything—life, money, relationships, your health, your family, your past, your present, your future—these thought-seeds are planted in the fertile soil of what we could call Infinite Intelligence, or God.

Your life then becomes a reflection of the thought-seeds you've planted in the "soil" of Infinite Intelligence. Therefore, your life is a reflection of the thoughts you consistently think.

You would think that, with the sheer number of books and programs in our industry that support this notion, by now we'd all know how to change our lives simply by repeating positive statements over and over. But all you have to do is look around to see that unfortunately, this is not the case (yet). The question is: *Why not?*

Your life is a reflection of the thoughts you consistently think.

The Missing Piece

Let's say, for example, that one of the changes you wanted was to earn more money. Because you had this goal, you began to study how to achieve it. You read books, attended seminars, and listened to traditional success teachers who told you that in order to change your life (that is, make more money), you must first change your thoughts about money.

Makes sense so far. You understand the truth of the statement, "As you sow, so shall you reap," which is simply another way of saying that your life is a reflection of the thoughts you consistently think (the thought-seeds you're planting).

You think back to childhood and recognize that perhaps you grew up experiencing a lack of money; therefore, you identified that the thought that's been holding you back is, *I don't have enough money.*

Now that you've identified the main thought that's been keeping you stuck, you realize that your next step is to *change that thought.* In other words, you decide to stop planting negative thought-seeds (that created a life you don't want), and start planting positive thought-seeds (that will, you hope, create the new life you do want).

Then you did what the traditional success teachers told you to do: started using positive statements or affirmations to change those old thoughts into new ones. Why? Because you're trying to change your life, so you need to change your thoughts, and so of course the way to do that is to change negative statements into positive statements.

For example, to overcome the negative thought of *I don't have enough money,* you started saying, writing, and repeating the positive statement: "I have enough money" or even "I am rich."

And because you're a good student, you did this over and over and over again. Dozens, hundreds, maybe thousands of times.

Then what happened?

Let's give it a try.

Right now, say to yourself, "I am rich."

Say it again—this time with emotion.

"I am *rich!*"

What just happened in your mind?

Did you hear something else in there?

Was it a voice that said something like, "Yeah, right!"?

• • •

So here it is, the key question I must ask you now:

Question: Do you believe your own affirmations?

Answer: The plain and simple truth is that many of us simply don't believe our own affirmations. We've been saying, writing, and repeating these positive statements over and over again for years; but for some reason, we just don't believe them.

And that lack of belief, which I call the *Belief Gap,* is the "something missing" in our old approach.

The Belief Gap

Whenever you're trying to change your life—for example, make more money, find a more fulfilling career, attract your soul mate, improve your health, lose weight, and so forth—what you're really trying to do is *create a new reality* for yourself. Let's illustrate that by saying that you want to go from your current reality to a new reality.

Perception is reality to the perceiver.

The funny thing about reality, though, is that *all reality is perceived reality.* Another way of saying that is: *perception is reality to the perceiver.*

For example, let's say you have a die-hard Boston Red Sox fan and a die-hard New York Yankees fan, and they're in the same room watching the Red Sox play the Yankees. (I have no idea why they're in the same room, but still.) Are these two people going to see the same game?

The answer is, of course, yes and no.

Yes, they are watching *the same set of circumstances* that occur on the field—a guy on one team gets a hit, someone on the other team strikes out, and so on.

But no, they are not watching the same game at all! That's because one of them will celebrate whenever "his" team gets a hit, while the other one will moan in pain. One of them will high-five his friends (who also root for "his" team) when "their" team wins, while the fan of the other one will mope around for days because "his" team lost.

That's why perception is reality to the perceiver.

Going back to our example, here's what's really happening when you're trying to change your life:

1. Right now you are living in what I call your **Current Perceived Reality (CPR).** In your CPR, you have what you have, you know what you know, you do what you do, and you are what you are. This is your Current Perceived Reality—and to you, your perception *is* reality. There is nothing else. It is your own little universe.

2. What you want is to be someplace else. You want to change something about your life (get a new result). For instance, you want to change your weight, your finances, your health, your relationships, your level of fame, your sphere of influence, your lifestyle, or any number of other things. That "someplace else" is what I call your **New Desired Reality (NDR).**

3. Between your CPR and your NDR lies what I call your **Belief Gap:** the space between where you perceive you are right now (your CPR) and what it will be like when you arrive "someplace else" (your NDR).

Here's a picture to illustrate what I'm talking about:

© and ™ Noah St. John

How big is your Belief Gap? That depends on a number of things: how long you've been in your CPR; how hard you think it will be to get to your NDR; how many of your friends tell you, "It's impossible," when you tell them your dreams; and so on.

Also, you probably have different Belief Gaps for different results you want to realize in your life. For example, you may think it's really hard to lose 20 pounds, but really easy to make an extra $10,000 a month. Or you may think losing 20 pounds is a piece of cake (pun intended), but to make an extra $10,000 a month is well nigh impossible!

Bottom line? Until you cross your individual Belief Gap for each result, outcome, or experience you want in your life, it will be very difficult for you to make the leap to reach the new life and create the new reality you desire.

How to Bridge the Belief Gap

Have you ever realized you were planting negative thought-seeds (for example, *I'm broke, I'm lonely, I can't lose weight, I'm unhappy*), decided you wanted something better, tried saying positive statements over and over again just like they told you to, and then had . . . absolutely nothing happen?

Me, too . . . and about a gazillion other people.

But why?

Were we incapable of thinking a positive thought, not smart enough, not motivated enough, not educated enough, or just not meant to be successful?

The answer is: none of the above.

The reason the traditional method did not give us the results we were hoping for is because we were trying to overcome the Belief Gap using only statements, since that's what we were told to do.

But your subconscious mind, the place where positive changes begin, responds automatically to something that's both simpler and more powerful than statements.

Your mind responds automatically to something that's both simpler and more powerful than statements.

However, since no one told you that before, you kept using a method that sometimes worked and sometimes didn't. It's like you have been working really hard trying to build a new house . . . but the only tool you were given was a chainsaw.

Well, I've got some exciting news that could very well change your life:

Rather than continuing to beat yourself up
for not getting the results you wanted,
let me introduce you to a method
that's both simpler and easier than
the one you've been using.

Now It's Your Turn

You've been trying to change your life by using statements to overcome your Belief Gap.

However, starting in the next chapter, you can start to change your life by asking a new kind of question.

What on Earth do I mean?

• ● •

CHAPTER 2

INTRODUCING AFFORMATIONS:

THE MISSING PIECE TO HAVING ABUNDANCE

"I don't pretend to have all the answers.
But the questions are sure worth thinking about."

— ARTHUR C. CLARKE

Did you see what just happened? I ended the last chapter with a question. And what did that do to your brain? Don't you really want to know what I mean by "asking a new kind of question"? Isn't your mind feverishly searching for the answer right now?

Are you ready to find out how and why this happens—and why your life is about to change as a result?

What Is a Question?

A *question* is an expression of inquiry that calls for a reply. When you ask a question, what happens?

For example, right now, you're probably thinking, *I don't know—what happens when I ask a question?*

Do you see that? When you ask a question, *your mind automatically begins to search for an answer.*

You can't help it. It's automatic. It happens without your volition. Searching for an answer to a question is perhaps the most basic and fundamental function of the human mind.

On that fateful morning of The Shower That Changed Everything, I realized that this simple truth of human consciousness may hold the answer to solving life's biggest problems. Here's what I mean. . . .

What Every Problem You'll Ever Face Really Is

No one likes problems. Most of us try to avoid, ignore, or get away from them. Some would argue that problems are the bane of human existence. But really, every problem you'll ever face is simply *a question that hasn't been answered yet.*

Any problem, from the trivial to the tremendous, is really a question searching for an answer. For example, here are a few serious global problems and their associated questions:

> Every problem is simply a question that hasn't been answered yet.

PROBLEM	QUESTION
Global warming	How can we stop destroying the planet and still live the prosperous lives we want?
Poverty	How can we equally distribute the world's enormous wealth so no one has to go without adequate food, clothing, and shelter?
Unemployment	How can we get all people working in jobs that produce wealth for themselves and help society function better?

Notice that I didn't say these were easy problems to solve. That's why we haven't found all the answers yet!

What about regular, everyday human problems? Here are some common problems that many people face, along with their related questions:

PROBLEM	QUESTION
Money	How can I make more money without sacrificing my family, my values, or my freedom?
Weight	How can I lose weight, be healthy, and still enjoy the foods I want?
Business	How can I grow my business and attract more customers without struggling?

As you can see, every problem is, at its root, a question (or series of questions) that hasn't been answered yet.

Let's say you wanted to solve a common problem that millions of people face every day, like how to make more money, lose weight, or be happier. One approach would be to use the traditional affirmation method by saying things like: "I am rich," "I am thin," "I am happy," and so on.

You may believe these statements, and you may not. However, your Belief Gap may be so wide that even though you *want* to believe these positive statements, you just don't. That's why many so people respond to statements like this with the "Yeah, right" response—and eventually give up on their dreams.

If you've been tempted to give up, let me show you something so powerful and yet so simple that the traditional success teachers skipped right over it on the way to breakfast this morning:

If you don't believe
your positive statements yet,
why not ask a question
that will change your life?

How You Create Your Life

The staggering realization I made in The Shower That Changed Everything on that fateful morning in April 1997 was that you create your life in two ways: by the statements you say to yourself and others, and by the questions you ask yourselves and others.

Traditional success teachers have focused a great deal of time and energy on telling you to change your statements. For millions of people, that method has worked . . . and for millions, it hasn't.

But until my discovery, no one had fully realized or shown how to harness the awesome power of what happens when you *change your internal and external questions.*

> You create your life by the statements you say to yourself and others and by the questions you ask yourself and others.

Your mind has what we could call an **automatic search function**—which means that when you ask a question, your mind automatically begins to search for an answer. (Psychologists have referred to this function of the human brain as the "embedded presupposition factor.")

For example, imagine if I were to ask you, "Why is the sky blue?" Do you know what your brain is doing right now? It's searching for the answer to that question. Notice that it did so without your telling it to. You didn't *try* to start searching for the answer. You didn't have to *make yourself* do it. In fact, your brain couldn't help it. Literally, you couldn't *not* do it!

This is often referred to as the Law of Sowing and Reaping, because you reap what you sow. Emerson called it "First Law" or the "Law of Attraction," which means that what you focus on—the thought-seeds you continually plant—will grow and bear fruit. (By the way, the answer to the question is that molecules in the Earth's atmosphere scatter blue light from the sun more than they scatter red light. Now you can impress your friends at parties!)

As we've seen, traditional success teachers have told you to change your thinking if you want to change your life. And that's quite correct. Yet even as far back as biblical times, we've been reminded, "You have not because you ask not," and "Ask and you shall receive."

If you change only the statements you say
without changing the questions you ask,
you're missing out on the most
simple, effective way to bridge
your Belief Gap—and change your life.

How a 13-Year-Old Girl Cured Her Compulsive Worrying

I got a phone call one day from Mary, a working mom from Wisconsin who had attended one of our seminars. The first words she said to me were, "Noah, your work has changed my life!" When I asked her what she meant, she told me the following story:

> After attending your seminar and learning how to use Afformations, I realized that if it could work for me, it could also work for my 13-year-old daughter Stefanie. She's a high achiever who gets all *A*'s in school, but she was also a chronic and compulsive worrier.
>
> Stefanie worried so much that she had developed severe sleeping problems. She'd lay awake many nights worrying, until finally she'd come into our bedroom and wake us from a sound sleep so we could comfort her.

We tried everything. We read to her. We prayed with her. We were even considering taking her to therapy. Still the worrying—and the sleepless nights—continued.

She would cry and ask me, "Why do I worry so much?" It broke my heart because I couldn't help my own daughter.

When I heard you teach Afformations, I realized that this was the answer I'd been praying for! I came back from your seminar and immediately taught Stefanie how to use Afformations.

She was as excited as I was! The questions we came up with for her were:

Why am I worry free?

Why do I enjoy a full night's sleep?

Why do I put my trust in God's hands?

Why do all my friends love me?

Why do I love me?

From the very first day she started using Afformations, Stefanie's worrying stopped! It was truly miraculous!

She also became much happier, is more relaxed, and seems to be at peace in her own skin. And you know how hard that can be for teenagers nowadays.

Your books were the first self-help books I've ever read that inspired me to actually *do* the exercises. Thank you, Noah, for making such a difference in our lives!

Mary then told me that not only did Afformations enable Stefanie to quit worrying, but they also helped Mary build her home-based business and attract more customers. She started telling all her friends about Afformations and using them in all areas of her life.

Then, when Mary's husband, Scott, told her that he wasn't passionate about his work any more, she began afforming, *Why is the right calling coming to Scott?* Within weeks, he landed his dream job. And get this: it was a position working at Stefanie's high school. That means this family used Afformations to gain more peace of mind, find more fulfillment at work, an increased income, and even enjoy more family time together. Now that's what I call afforming!

Empowering vs. Disempowering Questions

Most people are going through life asking a lot of disempowering questions without realizing it—then they wonder why they're not getting the results they dream of. Therefore, let's begin by examining the disempowering questions you're unconsciously asking right now, then learn how to consciously change your disempowering questions into Afformations, which are empowering questions.

What are *disempowering questions?* They're questions that do precisely that: they *disempower* you and effectively take away your power to act by focusing your mind on what you *don't* have, what you *can't* do, and who you are *not.*

Questions like, *Why am I so broke? Why doesn't anyone love me? How come I never have enough money? Why am I so fat?* and *Why can't I lose weight?* are examples of disempowering questions, because they cause you to believe you can't do the things you want to do in life.

Of course, no one goes around asking these negative questions on purpose. But you may be unconsciously asking disempowering questions like these without even realizing it.

That's why I'd like you to try something right now. I want you to say these common disempowering questions out loud, and see how you feel as a result. Ready?

- *Why don't I have enough money?*

- *Why am I so lonely?*

- *Why am I such a loser?*

- *Why am I so fat?*

- *Why am I so broke?*

- *Why do I never get the breaks that other people get?*

- *Why can't I do anything right?*

Did you do it? When you consciously ask disempowering questions, say them out loud, or even think them, it doesn't feel very good, does it?

As I explain in my seminars and mastermind programs, each of us is carrying around what I call a **Negative Reflection** in our subconscious mind— that negative inner voice that tells us we can't do anything right. The Negative Reflection always asks negative or disempowering questions like the ones listed above.

Disempowering questions take away your power to act.

The ultimate result of them is that you manifest what you focus on. In other words, when you ask yourself negative questions, you get negative results.

In your Afformations Journal, I want you to write the five most disempowering questions that your Negative Reflection asks you on a regular basis.

Yes, I mean right now.

These disempowering questions may have come from someone in your past, or perhaps you made them up on your own. Either way, it's vital that you know exactly what your own disempowering questions are so you can begin to turn them around. (Please write today's date next to the disempowering questions you write, because when you come back to your notes later, you'll see just how far you've come once you've been using The Afformations Method, even for a very short time.)

Please do this right now. I'll be right here when you get back.

• • •

Whew. Pretty bad, aren't they?

Are you ready to find a better way?

Empowering Questions—The Right Questions to Ask

Now that you've identified the disempowering questions you've been unconsciously asking, you're probably asking another question right now: "Okay, if those are the disempowering questions I've been asking, what are *empowering questions*—and how can I start asking those instead?"

I'm glad you asked!

Empowering questions are those that have precisely the opposite effect of their negative counterparts. While disempowering questions focus your mind on what you don't have, can't do, and are not—and therefore take away your power to act—empowering questions focus your mind what you *have,* what you *can* do, and who you *are.* In short, they unleash your ability to *take action* and express Who You Really Are.

The answers to empowering questions produce feelings of positive self-worth and ultimately lead to answers that tell the truth about Who You Really Are.

> Empowering questions unleash your ability to take action and express Who You Really Are.

Let's try something fun right now. I want you to change the five disempowering questions you just wrote into empowering questions. How do you do this? Simply reverse the negative question into a positive!

For example, let's say one of the disempowering questions you wrote was: *How come I never get the breaks other people get?*

Your empowering question might be: *Why am I so lucky?*

Or if one of the disempowering questions you wrote was: *Why am I so fat?*

Your empowering question could be: *Why is it so easy for me to lose weight?*

Got it? Grab your pen and change your five disempowering questions into empowering questions in your Afformations Journal. Are you ready to experience the Afformations difference? Go for it!

• • •

Pretty cool, huh? Did you notice something shift in your mind? What does it feel like? In your Afformations Journal right now, write the difference you feel from doing the first exercise to doing the second one.

• • •

Congratulations! You've just begun an amazing journey to your new abundant lifestyle. . . .

How an Insurance Salesman Increased His Income by 560 Percent in Less Than a Year

Brandon, an insurance salesman from Utah, had heard about Afformations from a friend and decided to invest in the home-study programs we offer. Here's what happened next, in Brandon's own words:

> After spending over a decade and more than $30,000 on everything from books, tapes, and seminars, to actually becoming certified as a Neuro-Linguistic Programming practitioner, what has happened to me as a result of using Afformations is nothing short of amazing!
>
> After going through Noah's home-study program, I realized that I was subconsciously asking myself a ton of disempowering questions that were stopping my growth—negative questions like *Why can't I get any new referrals?* and *Why can't I make more money?*
>
> I immediately started asking myself positive Afformations. First, I began asking, *Why do I get referrals every day?* Within four days, I had received *nine* new referrals to new clients. I had

never received that many referrals in such a short period of time!

Before I met Noah, my sales averaged between $1,500 and $2,000 per month. In the first 30 days of using Noah's program, *my sales tripled.* By the end of the year, my personal income had increased by *more than 560 percent,* and I was named Agent of the Year. I managed to do all this despite going through a painful divorce and mourning the loss of my grandmother.

After that first year, I realized I was ready to get back into a relationship. I began afforming: *Why am I so lucky to meet the perfect woman for me so quickly?*

In less than 40 days, I met a fantastic woman. But what's truly miraculous is that if we'd met just one week earlier, I wouldn't have been open to dating her, because I wanted someone over 21 years old (I was 27 at the time)—and we met just four days after her 21st birthday.

My advice to everyone reading this? Follow Noah's program—because it will change your life!

Why Are They Called Afformations?

I named the process of creating and asking empowering questions **The Afformations® Method.** But where did the word *Afformations* come from?

After my discovery in the shower, I realized that the process of asking empowering questions could completely revolutionize the fields of self-help and personal growth. I also decided to create a new word to describe this process, because I wanted people to more deeply understand how their thoughts and beliefs are forming their lives.

One of my favorite subjects in high school was Latin (yes, I was a geek long before they put the word *computer* in front of it), and after my breakthrough, I discovered that the word *affirmation* comes from the Latin word *firmare*, which means "to make firm."

I asked myself, "If affirmations are positive *statements*, what would be the perfect word to describe empowering *questions?*" After I asked the question, the answer came to me (of course!): I realized that when we ask questions—whether empowering or disempowering—we are really *forming* thought patterns, which then *form* our habits, which then *form* our very lives.

> What if you're making something *firm*, but it's in the wrong *form?*

The word *form* comes from the Latin word *formare*, which means "to form or give shape to." That's when it hit me: What if you're making something *firm*, but it's in the *wrong form?* That would be called, "Forming a life you *don't* want!"

That's when I realized why so many people have so much trouble overcoming their Belief Gap using only statements—even though they're trying to make something *firm*, they haven't yet *formed* their new belief structure or new habits. Seen in this new light, it's like trying to build a house without first pouring the foundation.

I realized that, before we make something *firm*, we first need to *form* questions that will change the thought-seeds we're sowing . . . which will change our thinking . . . change our beliefs . . . change our habits . . . and ultimately, change our lives.

And that's how the word—and the teaching of—Afformations was born.

(By the way, it's perfectly legitimate to invent a word to describe a new technology or a new way of looking at the universe. For example, remember the first time you heard the words *Internet, Google,* or even *computer?* Just a short time ago in human history, these words didn't exist, because the technology they describe didn't exist. There was no *context* for them and no meaning. Now we use these words every day! In this book, I'm teaching you *a new technology of the mind.* Hence, *Afformations*—a new word to describe a new technology of the mind and a new way of looking at the universe.)

Bottom Line? You're Already Doing This

In case you're still wondering if this really works, or thinking this is the nuttiest thing you've ever heard, let me offer you one final fact:

You're already using Afformations.

Thoughts like *Why am I so stupid?* or *Why can't I do anything right?* are simply negative Afformations. Negative, disempowering questions like these are really your Negative Reflection forming itself inside your mind, thereby forming your thinking, your behavior, and ultimately your life.

For example, I was speaking in Virginia doing one of our live seminars, when a young couple came up to me—literally jumping up and down with excitement! They said they'd heard me teach Afformations at the national convention for one of the world's largest direct-sales companies. Here's their story:

> Our dream was to qualify for the car our company offers as an incentive for sales performance. Since that was our goal, we'd been using affirmations for the past four years just as we'd been told: we made audios and listened to them over and over, repeated them all the time to each other, and placed them all over our refrigerator.
>
> We even hung affirmation signs in the shower to try to reach our goal . . . but all we got was a bunch of wet words!
>
> After hearing you speak about Afformations during your keynote speech at our national convention, we were very excited. We realized that Afformations really *are* the missing piece to having abundance, because they allowed us to bridge the gap between the positive statements we were saying and our own inner beliefs.
>
> We started asking each other our new, empowering questions, placed them all over our refrigerator, and talked about our new Afformations day after day.
>
> The results were absolutely amazing! We heard you speak at our national convention in July. By August, we realized we were doing a lot of things differently because of the Afformations we were using. And in September, our production had increased so much that we finally qualified for our first company car!
>
> In short, after four years of not reaching our goal, *we got the exact results we wanted in less than 90 days using Afformations.* Thank you, Noah!

This professional couple had been very committed to using the traditional method. They'd been saying their statements for over four years—now that's commitment! However, because they hadn't been able to connect the positive statements they were saying with their inner (real) beliefs, they weren't able to overcome their Belief Gap, and their subconscious negative programming hadn't allowed them to get the results they had hoped for.

Why not use your mind to create the life you do want, rather than one you don't?

Using Afformations, however, unleashed their inner power to search for creative ways to solve their problems—and the results spoke for themselves.

The power to re-create your life using Afformations lies within you and your miraculous, marvelous mind. In fact, since you're already using Afformations anyway, why not use them consciously to create the life you want, rather than using them unconsciously to create a life you don't?

By the way, if you still doubt the power of Afformations, there is a sentence that's 11 letters long that represents the genesis of science, religion, philosophy, mathematics, history, and every work of art in human history.

If you're still not sure whether Afformations will work for you, here is the question that has, in a very real sense, created human history:

Why am I alive?

• • •

In the next section of this book, I'll teach you the four steps to create empowering Afformations that will change your life and show you the way to a new, abundant lifestyle.

Are you ready?

• ● •

PART II

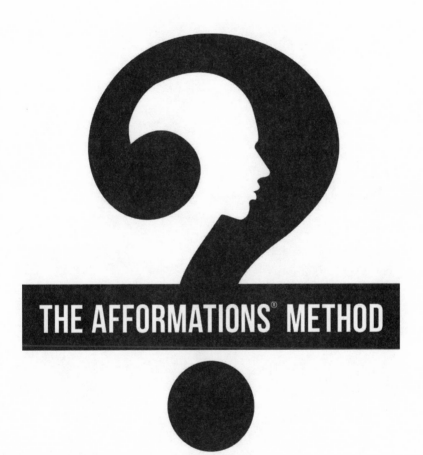

THE AFFORMATIONS® METHOD

STEP ONE: ASK

"If you can't answer, simplify the question."

— TOBA BETA

Afformations have helped countless people around the world to make more money, boost self-confidence, improve personal relationships, be happier and healthier, quit bad habits like smoking and overeating, and enjoy a deeper connection with God.

I've taught these four steps to countless groups around the world—from business owners in Australia to working moms in New York, to direct sales professionals in Dallas to multimillionaire CEOs in Florida. And in thousands upon thousands of cases, these four simple steps have changed people's lives for the better.

That's why I hope you will use these four simple steps of The Afformations Method to design and create a more abundant lifestyle for yourself and your family, and then *take action* to make it a reality.

Here, then, is Step One of The Afformations Method:

The Afformations Method
Step One: Ask Yourself What You Want.

If you were in New York City and wanted to take a road trip to meet a friend in Los Angeles, which approach would you choose?

1. Pick a specific location, date, and time for your meeting; figure out the fastest route to take; and then start on your journey—giving yourself enough time to allow for the inevitable delays, detours, and roadblocks.

2. Jump in your car and drive west until you hit the ocean, drive up and down the coast until you find the city of Los Angeles, and then ask everyone you meet to tell you where your friend is.

You'd pick the first option, right? After all, it is the far more efficient approach and produces a near-guaranteed result of meeting up with your friend.

Why is it, then, that most people choose the second approach when it comes to pursuing their dreams and living their lives? Armed with only a vague idea of what they want and how to get there, they wander through life, hoping against hope that they will reach their destination.

This approach doesn't work for success any better than it works for a cross-country trip. Setting goals gives you a clear destination, the focus to keep you on track, and the awareness to guide your choices and actions.

That's why the first step in The Afformations Method is to *ask yourself what you really, really want.* You can use goals you've already written, or you can start from scratch. It's completely up to you.

Why Goal Setting Is Not Enough

Okay, I know you've heard every personal-growth guru on the planet say things like "Set your goals" and "If you believe, you can achieve." I bet you've even tried setting your goals and encountered some frustrations along the way—like, oh, I don't know, *not* reaching your goals?!

That means there must be something missing here, right? As I'm sure you've guessed by now—yep, there is.

What's been missing in our industry is a way to overcome the simple, fundamental truth that's staring us right in the face:

Most people don't believe they can reach their goals.

Many people in our industry would rather not talk about this nagging little detail. Yet the fact remains that, even though we've heard the advice to "set our goals" a thousand times, the vast majority of people simply don't believe they can reach the goals they set in the first place.

That's why I want to introduce you to something that may open your eyes to a new truth about yourself. . . .

Introducing the D.B.A.R. Cycle

Here is a simple four-part diagram that shows how your life works. (I know, how's that for a statement!)

We start with *desire*. Everything we human beings do starts with desire. For instance, in the ancient Hindu text known as the Rig Veda, desire is called "the first seed of mind." Everything we do springs forth from a seed of desire.

Let's say you want something—whether it's a new car, a new house, or a ham sandwich for lunch. Everything you and I wish for, hope for, dream of, fantasize about, crave, aspire to, set our sights on, and want (or think we want) is simply another way of saying we have a desire.

A desire is a destination—someplace we want to go. A destination is a goal—something we want to achieve. Therefore, your desires reveal what your goals are.

A desire can be as simple as a ham sandwich or as lofty as world peace. Yours will reflect what you want, your priorities, and your values. But mostly, they'll reveal what you believe you can actually achieve.

Your desires reveal what you believe you can actually achieve.

The next step is *belief.* Let me show you what I mean. . . .

Could You Get a Hit?

Imagine that you were in a baseball game, and you were going up to bat against a major-league pitcher. How confident would you be that you had a chance of getting a hit?

Now, I'm sure there are some great athletes reading this book; but most of us are perfectly aware that we have about as much chance of getting a hit against a major-league pitcher as an ice-cream cone's chance of surviving an August afternoon in Phoenix, Arizona (not much).

We have a desire (to get a hit), but we don't have the *belief* that we can actually do it. Therefore, we have a Belief Gap, which I showed you in Part I.

Because we have a Belief Gap (for example, your inner self telling you, *There's no way I can get a hit!*), what would your *actions* be?

More than likely, your actions would be tentative and fearful, since you're certain that you can't succeed in this situation. And if your actions are tentative and fearful, what do you think your *results* will be? Exactly: more than likely, not getting a hit.

When you put it all together, it looks like this:

Desire: *I want to hit the ball.*

Belief: *But there's no way I can do this.*

Action: Either not taking a swing, or doing so tentatively and fearfully.

Result: Not getting a hit.

Why Most People Quit

We all have desires—whether it's the desire for money, fame, or a new car; to lose weight, be healthy, or have better relationships; to find the love of your life; or simply the desire to be happy.

Let's imagine that you're thinking about this thing that you want (and remember, we're not only talking about material things like money, cars, and houses, but also intangible and very important things like health, love, and happiness).

When you want something, but don't believe you can actually have it, what will your *actions* be?

What happens in the moment you think about this thing that you desire? For many people, what happens is, deep down, they don't believe they can have it, do it, or be it.

When you want something, but don't believe you can actually have it, do it, or be it, what are your *actions* going to be regarding that thing? Exactly!

- *Tentative*
- *Fearful*

- *Anticipating failure*

- *Done with the belief that it won't work out*

- *Lacking belief in yourself*

- *Done with the belief that someone else can do it better than you can*

Is it any wonder why most people quit before they get what they really, really want?

> Most people have trained themselves to not believe in themselves.

But you see, the problem is not just that most people quit before they fulfill their desires. That problem is that, because most individuals have been beaten down and beaten up by life, they have *trained themselves to not believe in themselves.*

How to Believe in Yourself

Now I'd like you to imagine that you are in that same baseball game. But this time, instead of going up to bat against a major-league pitcher, you are going up to hit a ball off of a tee. (So you can picture it more easily, a tee is a stationary gizmo that the ball is placed on near home plate to help children hone their hitting skills.)

How sure are you that you can hit the ball now?

It's clear that most of us would feel pretty confident if we were going up to hit a ball that's literally teed up for us. So here's the equation this time:

Desire: *I want to hit the ball.*

Belief: *I can do this!*

Action: Swinging for the fences.

Result: Getting a hit!

See the difference?

Because most people *don't believe* that they can actually reach their goals (fulfill their desires, get what they want, manifest their dreams), they don't *feel* confident; because they don't feel confident, they don't take much *action*; because they don't take much action, they don't get the *result* they wanted; and because they don't get the result they wanted, they don't *feel* confident. This is what I call the *downward death spiral.*

Of course, not everything in life is as easy as hitting a ball off of a tee. However, imagine that you have individuals who are caught in the downward death spiral of not believing in themselves, not taking much action, and not getting the results they want. Now imagine that they're told to do an exercise such as setting their goals. Can you now see why they'll most likely be going through the motions instead of actively participating and *believing* that they can reach their destination? Can you also see that this is the very reason why most "set your goals" advice is an exercise in futility?

> Most "set your goals" advice is an exercise in futility.

That's why it's time to go back to the beginning—and determine if you believe you can even reach your goals in the first place.

It's Time to Raise the D.B.A.R.

Please understand that it's not wrong to ask yourself what you want and then set your goals. In fact, it's essential. However, if you don't also have the belief that you can actually reach your goals in the first place, trying to set them is effectively a waste of your time.

That's why, with The Afformations Method, I'm now handing you a proven, step-by-step process to not merely "set your goals," but more important, to actually *believe* that you can reach your goals and achieve what you really, really want in the first place.

In other words, I believe you can hit the ball. And by the end of this book, so will you!

Here's What I Want You to Do Now

1. Ask yourself what you really, really want in the Ten Major Areas of Life. This is the first step to uncover your true desires. (Everything starts with desire, remember?) To help you do this, in Part III of this book I've given you more than 400 specific Afformations to assist you in reaching your goals in the Ten Major Areas of Life. These areas are:

- Health and Well-Being
- Money and Abundance
- Building Self-Confidence
- Work and Career
- Love and Intimacy
- Family and Relationships
- Conquering Fear
- Overcoming Bad Habits
- Spirituality
- Life and Happiness

2. As you begin asking yourself what you really, really want, capture your desires in writing. To paraphrase the old saying: a mental note isn't worth the paper it's written on. Sure, you can daydream, you can doodle . . . but since you're taking the time and making the emotional commitment to read this book, don't you owe it to yourself to also commit your desires, goals, and dreams to writing? That's why I want you to record your desires in your Afformations Journal.

3. Be as specific as possible when capturing your desires. Remember our example of driving from New York to Los Angeles and making a specific plan versus just hoping for the best. Isn't your life worth more than a cross-country trip?

For example, here are some things you could list that you want to do, achieve, or experience in the area of Health and Well-Being:

I want to . . .

- . . . lose 20 pounds by (a specific date)
- . . . fit into my skinny jeans again
- . . . start eating healthier foods
- . . . cut out unhealthy foods
- . . . get better, more restful sleep
- . . . feel more confident about my body

These are specific, measurable, tangible goals. Remember, a goal is simply a destination. Just like when you're driving, you normally wouldn't just hop in the car, start driving, and hope you arrive somewhere sometime. You usually have a specific destination in mind, even if it's just down the street to the grocery store.

Therefore, make sure you write at least one goal or destination for each area, because it's important to know where you're going. There's no hard-and-fast rule for how many goals you can have; however, keep in mind that your brain can handle a lot more than you think (more on this later).

Now let's go to the next step of The Afformations Method—the one that's about to change your life!

• ● •

CHAPTER 4

STEP TWO: AFFORM

"Take the attitude of a student: never be too big to ask questions, never know too much to learn something new."

— OG MANDINO

If this were a traditional success book, the next thing I would tell you is that after you've "set your goals" (asked yourself what you want), you should start making a plan to get there. After all, that sounds logical, doesn't it? Just like our cross-country road trip, once you know your destination, you'd just pack up your stuff and head out, right?

Well, that approach *would* work if not for one tiny little detail: that annoying but inescapable fact that most people don't believe they can reach their goals in the first place.

Bottom line: what's been missing in our industry is a specific, proven, simple method to overcome the Belief Gap. Well, here it is:

The Afformations Method
Step Two: Form a New Question That Assumes That What You Want Is Already True.

The second step of The Afformations Method is to start creating empowering questions that *assume* that what you want is already so, has already happened, or is true!

This is the key to creating Afformations that will change your life.

How This Works

Your life is a reflection of the thought-seeds you plant and give energy to. More precisely, your life is a reflection of the unconscious assumptions you make about life and your relationship to it.

For example, if you grew up in an environment where there wasn't much money, you would probably assume that making money is hard, and that's just the way it is. And because you made this assumption unconsciously, you probably wouldn't even realize that you're holding on to it in the first place.

If you could find a mechanism that could record the thought-seeds you're planting on the inside and play them back to you on the outside, it might sound something like this:

- *Why am I so broke?*

- *Why don't I have enough money?*

- *How come I'm not more successful?*

- *How come I can never get ahead?*

- *Why do other people have so much more money than I do?*

Well, a mechanism *does* exist that records and reflects your subconscious thought-seeds. That mechanism is called *your life!*

This Is Your Life

There is a mechanism that records and reflects your subconscious beliefs. That mechanism is called *your life.*

So here you are, unknowingly asking yourself these negative questions, which lead to disempowering assumptions, which lead to you not believing you can reach your goals. What do you think the answers would be to the negative questions in the example I just gave you?

The answers would be things showing up in your life that reflect the disempowering questions you've been unconsciously asking. For example, if you've been unknowingly asking, *Why am I so unhappy?* the answers will show up as you being unhappy, no matter how many good things happen to you.

If you've been unconsciously asking, *Why don't I have enough money?* the answers will show up as your lack of money, no matter how hard or how long you work.

And if you've been unwittingly asking, *Why can't I lose weight?* the answer will show up as your not being able to lose weight, no matter how many diet and exercise programs you try.

Here's a chart to show you what I mean:

What You've Been Unconsciously Asking (Your Disempowering Assumptions)	How It Shows Up In Your Life
Why am I so unhappy?	You are unhappy most of the time.
Why am I so broke?	You find a way to not have money, even when money comes in.
Why can't I lose weight?	You find it hard to lose weight, no matter what you try.
Why can't I do anything right?	You focus on what you do wrong and ignore all the things you do right.

I call these *dassumptions*—a portmanteau of *disempowering* and *assumptions*. When you carry around these dassumptions, your life becomes a reflection of them. That's why all of the goal setting in the world won't work when this is the case—because you simply don't believe that you can reach your goals in the first place.

Reversing the Curse

When you do Step Two of The Afformations Method, you will take what has been unconscious (hidden) and make it conscious (visible), and in the process turn beliefs that have been negative (disempowering) into ones that are positive (empowering).

Let's reverse all the negative questions we've just looked at. They now would look something like this:

- *Why am I so happy?*
- *Why do I have enough money?*
- *Why is it so easy for me to lose weight?*
- *Why am I enough?*

These questions may seem unfamiliar (even down-right bizarre!) to you right now. But what if, just for a moment, you let yourself accept those questions as being true for you?

Wouldn't you have a life that's different from the average person's—a life that's different from the one you have now?

Your Quality of Life Depends on Just These Two Things

The quality of your life depends on just two things: the quality of your communication with the world *inside* of you, and the quality of your communication with the world *outside* of you.

When you follow Step Two, you will begin to change the quality of communication with the world inside of you. You will begin to ask yourself empowering questions and stop asking yourself disempowering ones.

Then, if you follow the remaining steps in The Afformations Method, you will start to

> The quality of your life depends on just two things: the quality of your communication with the world *inside* of you, and the quality of your communication with the world *outside* of you.

change the quality of communication with the world outside of you. This is the fastest, most effective way I've ever seen to change the quality of your communication with both your inside and outside worlds and thereby change your life.

For example, I got this e-mail from a client in England named Kaisha:

> Dear Noah,
>
> Once again, I have to say thank you!
>
> I have been afforming for 18 months now, but I never used them on money until I read one of your recent online updates.
>
> I was scared I might lose my home if I didn't earn more money. I afformed, *Why have I doubled my income?*
>
> It's less than a month, and my sales figures have tripled. Thank you!

I wrote to Kaisha a short time later to congratulate her and ask if I could share her story. Her reply:

> Of course! Just add that I have just been offered a new job at *double* my current salary!

Why Ask Why?

One of the most common questions I'm asked about Afformations is, "Why do they all start with the word *why?*" Good question!

Two basic forces govern human behavior: the *why* and the *how*. The why is your *motive* for doing something. The how is your *method* of doing it.

I often ask my coaching clients, seminar audiences, and mastermind students the following question: Which do you think is more powerful, the why or the how?

To answer that question, let me ask you another one: have you ever noticed that you can know *how* to do something, but never actually *do* it?

For example, there are hundreds of things you could do right now that you choose not to—run down the street naked, hug a cactus, or pick a fight with Chuck Norris (please don't try any of these!).

You have the how of doing these things (meaning you *could* do them if you wanted to), but you don't have the why of doing them (meaning you really don't *want* to do them).

Therefore, motive always trumps method, which means the why always trumps the how—and that is why Afformations start with the word *why*.

There's another reason Afformations start with *why*. Let's say you afform, *Why am I so rich?* Your mind immediately seeks to answer the question, which means you actually force it to focus on all the things you have.

But what if you were to ask yourself the question, "How did I get so rich?" Your mind would most likely be stumped, because you're asking it to discover the method by which you got rich before you believe you actually are. It would probably reply with something like, "What are you talking about? I don't know."

> The why always trumps the how.

There's absolutely nothing wrong with how questions. When you're trying to accomplish any goal, you definitely need to know how to do it.

The problem is that your mind can often get stuck on the how of doing something. For example, if you keep asking yourself, "How did I do this?" and "How did I do that?" it does not activate the embedded presupposition factor of your brain as Afformations do.

In short: Afformations are a specific form of empowering question that start with the word *why*. When you ask questions that assume that *what you want is already true*, you will activate that part of your brain that will seek to make it so. And that is what will unleash your hidden power to take action and change your life.

The Essence of Afformations

At its essence, Step Two of The Afformations Method is to ask yourself: "Why is [what I want] true in my life now?"

Why does this work? Because of your brain's embedded presupposition factor: when you ask a question, either internally or externally, your brain is wired to search for the answer. You can ask disempowering questions, or you can ask empowering ones. The choice is yours.

Here's What I Want You to Do Now

1. Go through your list you wrote for what you want in the Ten Major Areas of Life from Step One. You did do this, right? If not, go back and do it now. You have to know where you want to go if you want to get there!

2. Take what you want in each area and form an empowering question that assumes that what you want is already true or has already happened. For example, if what you want is to lose 20 pounds by a certain date, then your Affirmation might be: *Why did I lose 20 pounds by* [date]*?*

If what you want is to bring in more money for your business, your Affirmation could be: *Why did I start bringing in more money for my business?*

If you want to overcome a bad habit—for example, quit smoking—you can afform: *Why is it so easy for me to quit smoking?*

3. Study Part III of this book for specific Afformations to use in each Area of Life for your specific situation. I'll give you hundreds of examples of empowering Afformations in Part III. You'll notice that there are many different forms of empowering questions that will work for many different situations. Here's what I mean:

- "Why is it so easy for me to . . . ?"
- "Why am I . . . ?"
- "Why did I . . . ?"
- "Why do I have . . . ?"
- "Why do I love . . . ?"

Because there are an infinite number of questions you can ask, use these examples as starting points for your own new, empowering Afformations.

Now let's go to the all-important, not-to-be-missed Step Three of The Afformations Method!

• ● •

STEP THREE: ACCEPT

"Question everything. Learn something. Answer nothing."

— EURIPIDES

Once you've determined what you want (Step One) and formed new, empowering questions around that desire (Step Two), the next one must be to find all the answers to your questions, right?

Well, no. This is counterintuitive, but the point of using Afformations is not to answer the new questions you're asking. The point is to use your mind in a new way—to focus on what you *have* instead of what you *lack*.

That's why Step Three of The Afformations Method is:

> The purpose of Afformations is to focus on what you *have* instead of what you *lack*.

**The Afformations Method
Step Three: Accept the Truth
of Your New Questions.**

To demonstrate what I mean, here's a story that I received from John Adams of The Golden Key Ministry in Phoenix, Arizona:

> Dear Noah,
>
> I want to tell you a true story about my friends Sam and Shirley, two people to whom I taught The Afformations Method when I first read your Afformations book.
>
> Shirley had been accepted into the ministerial program at Unity in Missouri, so they planned to sell their home and move to Kansas City. They put their home on the market in early April with no results. People would come and look, but no one was buying.
>
> On Saturday, May 5, Sam and Shirley told me about their lack of a buyer for their home.
>
> Because they needed to leave in early June, they were getting nervous and wanted my advice. I suggested they go through every room in their home, bless it, and begin afforming, *Why is this house now easily sold to the right party for the right price?*
>
> That was Saturday. The next afternoon, a couple came and looked at the house. On Tuesday, they made an offer that was too low. Sam and Shirley kept their Afformation going and made a higher counteroffer—which was accepted on Tuesday afternoon!
>
> Everything went through quickly, and the deal closed on May 31. Sam and Shirley are now happily living in Missouri as true Afformers!

How Your Brain Is Like Google

Google is the world's most popular search engine. When you type a word or phrase into its search function, what you're really doing is asking a question: "Hey Google, can you find the answer to this question for me?" It then automatically performs a search to answer what you asked.

Your mind works just like this. When you ask yourself a question—whether empowering or disempowering—your mind automatically begins to search for the answer.

However, there's one big difference between your brain and Google: Google can't change the questions that it's asked. After you enter your query, Google can't reply, "Nah, I don't feel like answering that question right now; I'm going to answer this other question instead!" That's because Google is a software program designed by human beings; it does not have a conscious choice.

> You can choose to ask empowering or disempowering questions. Your brain will find an answer either way.

But *you* do. You are a human being. You have the choice of what questions you are going to ask at any given moment. You can decide, right now, to ask an empowering or disempowering question. Your brain will find the answer either way.

If you go around asking negative questions such as, *Why can't I do anything right? Why am I so broke?* and *Why am I so fat?*—whether you're asking these questions consciously or subconsciously—your brilliant brain will find the answers. And guess what? You'll feel as if you never do anything right, are broke, and are quite overweight.

Ironically, these beliefs will be true for you even if you're the smartest person in the world, have plenty of money, and are, to the outside observer, thin. (Yes, it is possible to feel stupid when you're smart, to feel broke when you have lots of money, and to feel fat when you're thin. I know this because I've mentored and coached many highly intelligent people who had completely convinced themselves of these untruths.)

Even if you don't consciously realize that you're asking yourself disempowering questions—since you're doing it at the subconscious level—your mind will still find reasons to make them true for you.

How to Use Your Brilliant Brain

But there's good news in all of this. In fact, there's great news!

You are a human being with a human brain, which means that you have a *choice*. You're able to choose what to think, what to say, and what to do. Because you have a choice, at any moment—*even at this very moment*—you have complete control to make these decisions.

This is one of the most miraculous aspects of your brilliant brain—you can change the questions you're asking any time you want!

Even if you've been asking yourself disempowering questions for months, years, and even decades, you can choose *right now* to change the questions you're asking.

Once you start using Afformations,
you never have to go back
to asking disempowering questions again.

How to Give Yourself to the Question

When I tell my coaching clients and mastermind students to "accept the truth of your new questions," they often ask me what that means. Here are four simple ways to give yourself to your new, empowering Afformations and accept them as true. You can:

1. Read them
2. Write them
3. Say them
4. Listen to them

These are the four modes of human communication. *Giving yourself to the question* means using all of these to accept the truth of your new questions.

> How many negative thoughts about yourself have you had in your lifetime?

Then my clients will ask me, "Which mode works the fastest?" (What they're really asking is, "Which of these should I spend the most time doing?")

While all four are essential, my experience with clients has shown that the one that produces the fastest results is listening.

Why would listening produce the fastest results? Think about it this way: how many negative thoughts have you had about yourself in your lifetime? A billion? A trillion? Could we even count that high?

Most of us could hardly count the number of negative thoughts we've had about ourselves. When you think these things, you're effectively "listening" to these negative thoughts in your head (that is, your Negative Reflection).

Therefore, when you listen to empowering Afformations, you will begin to drown out that negative voice and stop giving power to it. That's why I invented *iAfform Audios.*

iAfform Audios are empowering Afformations set to inspiring music that you can listen to anytime, anywhere. *iAfform Audios* will help you flip the abundance switch in your brain and manifest your desires while you're busy doing other things.

> The more you listen to empowering Afformations, the faster you'll drown out your Negative Reflection.

For example, you can listen to your *iAfform Audios* while you're eating or exercising, working or playing, in the car, on your laptop, or in your office. Many of my clients even listen to them while they sleep!

Because of the demand from clients around the world, I've created many different *iAfform Audios* for all areas of life, including:

- Ultimate Self-Confidence
- Ultimate Wealth
- Easy Weight Loss
- Deep Blissful Sleep
- Live Your Life Purpose
- . . . and many more

For example, Chris, a financial expert from Canada, writes:

> Noah, I listened to your *Ultimate Wealth iAfform Audio* for three weeks and just closed my first million-dollar client!

Michael from Germany sent me this amazing story:

Hi Noah,

I've bought every *iAfform Power Pack* you have. You might be wondering why I have gone Afformation crazy, but your Afformations changed my life in a few minutes on June 29, 2011.

I used to be a chronic procrastinator and had great resistance for the words *job, work,* and *working.* I also thought I was unable to be, do, or have anything: money, to keep a job, and so on, and my self-confidence was nonexistent. I did not realize that until I started using your *iAfform Wealth Power Pack.* In one night, in just a few minutes, there were *big* changes.

After listening to your free *60-Second iAfform Stress Buster*—which I placed on repeat and used for five minutes with the super result of total calm—I made the big leap of buying every one of your Power Packs at **iAfform.com.**

When I came across your work, my wife Silvia and I had our divorce papers on the desk, waiting to be signed. Then I shared your Afformations with her, and now we are best friends and in love again. We also have a list of 26 Afformations that we write every morning and read every chance we get throughout the day. It's a three-month commitment.

I also would like to get certified as one of your coaches, and I hope it's soon. Thank you, Noah, for changing our lives!

I encourage you to try *iAfform Audios* by downloading my free *60-Second iAfform Stress Buster* at **www.iAfform.com**—yes, using Afformations, you can bust your stress in 60 seconds or less! (See also your Free Bonus Gift at the back of this book.)

Here's What I Want You to Do Now

1. Take out your list of Afformations you wrote in Step Two. Remember, this all started with Ask Yourself What You Want (Step One). Then we went to Create Empowering Afformations (Step Two). If you haven't done these steps yet, now's the time to do them!

2. Take each Afformation and use the four modes of human communication to accept the truth of your new questions. This means you can:

- Read your new Afformations.
- Write them.
- Say them.
- Listen to them.

Let's say that you want to lose weight. You can:

- Read the health Afformations I've given you in the chapter on Health and Well-Being in this book.

- Write the ones that apply to your specific situation in your Afformations Journal.

- Say them out loud to yourself or with a friend.

- Listen to the *Ultimate Health iAfform Audio* available at **www.iAfform.com**.

- Create your own customized iAfform Audio in your own voice, using the specific Afformations and music of your choice at **www.Afformware.com.**

3. Repeat this process for as many different Afformations as you want, in as many areas of your life as you wish.

4. Repeat this process as often as necessary until you install your new, empowering beliefs. Some Afformations will be easier for you to believe, while others will take more time to bridge your Belief Gap. Don't rush the process. Baby steps are what are called for here.

• • •

This brings us to the fourth and final step of The Afformations Method—the one you absolutely must do if you want to manifest the results you want . . .

• ● •

CHAPTER
6

STEP FOUR: ACT

"Funny how 'question' contains the word 'quest' inside it, as though any small question asked is a journey through briars."

— CATHERYNNE VALENTE

Right now you are making hundreds, perhaps thousands, of unconscious assumptions about life and your relationship to it. These assumptions form the basis of how you go through life—positively or negatively, confidently or hesitantly, from love or from fear. However, the problem is that we usually don't recognize our own assumptions.

For example, let's say one of your unconscious assumptions is, *Things always work out for the best for me.* If you hold that assumption, what will your actions be? More than likely, your actions will be confident, your posture will be self-assured, and you will tend to persist even in the face of temporary failure.

But what if you hold the opposite assumption? What if you unconsciously believe, *How come things never work out for me?* What will your actions be then? If you hold this assumption, your actions will be hesitant, your posture will be one of defeat, and you will tend to give up at the first sign of resistance or rejection. In other words, your actions will be based on hesitancy, fear, and the belief of "Why even bother?"

That's why Step Four, the final step of The Afformations Method, is:

The Afformations Method
Step Four: Take New Actions Based on Your New Assumptions about Life.

The D.B.A.R. Cycle Concluded

Remember earlier when I introduced you to The D.B.A.R. Cycle? Well, here's "the rest of the story" . . .

We began with *desire:* you want something.

Next comes *belief:* you either believe that you can be/do/have that thing, or you don't.

Then comes *action:* your actions are based on your belief. If you believe that you *can't* be/do/have the thing you desire, you won't take much action, which means you probably won't get the thing you desire, which means you'll prove yourself right.

However, if you believe that you *can* be/do/have the thing you desire, you'll *take action,* and keep taking action, for as long as it takes!

But then what happens? When you have a desire, believe, and take action, that means you always get everything you want, right?

Right?

(Crickets chirping)

That would be, ah, no.

I know that many people in our industry don't like to talk about this, but the fact is that we have all had the experience of desiring something, really believing we were going to get it, taking action, and then . . . not getting it.

Whether it was the date with the pretty girl, the winner's trophy at the athletic event, to lose 20 pounds, to land that big client, or whatever it was, you and I have both had plenty of disappointments, setbacks, failures, and things not go our way—even when we did everything right.

What this means, then, is that after *desire, belief,* and *action* comes the final step: *result.* You want something, you believe something, you do something, and then something happens.

Desired Results vs. Undesired Results

However (and this is one of the more frustrating parts about life), there are two kinds of results we can experience: *desired results* and *undesired results.*

Desired results are when you get what you wanted: you got the date, you won the trophy, you lost the weight, you landed the client, and so on. *Undesired results,* on the other hand, are when you don't get what you wanted.

Now, if this were a typical success book, I'd say something like, "Work really hard, and you'll always get what you want!" But you and I both know that's not always the way it works. Sometimes you can work really, really hard and then not get the result you were hoping for. Of course, the opposite can happen, too: sometimes the very thing you wanted drops right in your lap when you're least expecting it!

Let me tell you a true story. Once upon a time, my friend Jack Canfield had an idea for a book that would uplift people's spirits. As he was meditating, the name *Chicken Soup for the Soul* came to him, so that's what he decided to call the book. He and his co-author Mark Victor Hansen started shopping their book to every publisher they could find, hoping to get it published.

What do you think happened at the first publisher they went to? "Chicken Soup for the *what?* Ridiculous!" Door slammed in their faces. (I'm exaggerating for effect here, but the point is, they experienced what's politely called a *rejection.*)

The second publisher? *Slam!* Same result. The third publisher? *Slam!* Same result. And the fourth and the fifth and the sixth and . . . you get the idea.

Let's pause and look at what's happening in this story. Jack had a *desire:* to get his book published. He had *belief:* he believed he would find a publisher for his book. He and Mark took *action:* they kept pitching their book idea.

And they kept getting *results* all right. The problem was that they were all *undesired* results: one rejection after another.

How many undesired results do you think they got before they got their desired result? Ten, twenty, maybe thirty rejections? *One hundred and forty-four.* That's right: they received an undesired result—namely, the answer no—144 times in a row. On the 145th try, they finally got their desired result: their first yes. The rest, of course, is publishing history.

How many of us can honestly say that we would have kept going after experiencing that many undesired results?

How Your Assumptions Form Your Life

You are continually forming assumptions about life and your relationship to it, but most of them are unconscious. As a result, the majority of your actions are governed by assumptions that you may have formed years, even decades ago.

For example, if you grew up experiencing a lack of love, support, or opportunity, you might have formed unconscious assumptions like, *I'll never be very successful* or *I'm not good enough* or *Why can't I catch a break?* If those are your unconscious assumptions (beliefs), your actions will tend to be tentative, fearful, and anticipating failure—and your results will tend to be less than desirable.

On the other hand, what if you grew up experiencing an abundance of love, support, and opportunity? What then would your unconscious assumptions about life be?

Most likely, something similar to, *I can live the life I choose* or *There's plenty of opportunity out there, I just have to go out and get it!*

The problem is, of course, that most of us did not grow up experiencing an abundance of love, support, or opportunity. In fact, the vast majority of human beings grow up in an environment of not enough— not enough love, not enough support, not enough money, and not enough opportunity. That's why most human beings have formed negative, disempowering assumptions about their lives—and why their actions and results naturally follow.

Your life is a reflection of your assumptions.

However, there's some wonderful news. No matter what happened in the past, no one can force you to think certain thoughts. You, and you alone, control your thoughts, beliefs, and actions.

If you continue to unconsciously ask yourself, *How come I can never get ahead?* your actions (or lack thereof) will spring from that negative assumption. But if you decide, right now, to change your assumptions by changing your Afformation to, perhaps: *Why is it so easy for me to succeed?*—and then change your actions accordingly— you have made a conscious decision to change your life.

The *Chicken Soup for the Soul* story I just told is a perfect illustration of this principle. Neither Jack nor Mark grew up with lots of money or opportunity. Both came from very humble beginnings. Yet they made a conscious choice that they were not going to be defined by their past.

They had a desire, they believed, and they took action . . . and kept taking action, even in the face of 144 undesired results (rejections). Because they persevered, even in the face of all those undesired results, they finally got the result they desired.

Remember that the point of The Afformations Method is not to find the answer to your questions. Since you are now going to be forming positive questions that assume that what you want is already true, your mind will work to find a way to make it so.

Can you see how this process must, if you let it, change your life?

How Afformations Saved Amy's Life

Since I began teaching Afformations in 1997, not a single day goes by that I don't receive grateful e-mails, cards, and messages from people around the world who tell me incredible stories of how using Afformations has changed their lives.

Here's one of the most powerful stories I've received:

> Hi Noah,
> I wanted to thank you for what you're doing. I believe your work saved my life.
> I had always been able to pay all of my bills on time, and I had excellent credit that I was proud of. But one day, I lost my job, found myself unable to pay my bills, and eventually my credit was ruined.

I began to have constant chest pain and panic attacks and a debilitating feeling of terror that I couldn't shake off. I had no job, and I couldn't see how I could even start looking for a job with such a state of mind.

I was suicidal. I had to write myself a note that said, "Just for today, I will not kill myself." I knew I couldn't really kill myself and leave my husband alone in this mess, but I wanted to be free of it all so badly that I couldn't get the thought of suicide out of my head.

A friend e-mailed me your link with the information about your online course. I'd read about 20 self-help books and courses over the last two years and thought, *I can't possibly read another book or do another course.*

But then I read your free chapters, and I so agreed with everything you said that I decided to buy your Afformations System (home-study course).

I read your Chapter 4 about how to create empowering Afformations. Instantly, I felt a tremendous sense of peace wash over me.

I had been completely unable to sleep, rest, or escape my feelings of panic. I would lie awake all night, my heart racing with anxiety, while my husband slept.

Following your advice in Chapter 4, I immediately wrote an Afformation to myself that read, *Why is it so easy for me to sleep well at night?*

That very night I was able to sleep peacefully again, and my anxiety disappeared.

I have many more Afformations that are working well for me, and I'm on my way back to feeling as I did before.

Your work saved me an enormous amount of suffering and loss—mentally, materially, spiritually, and physically.

There aren't enough words to describe my feelings of gratitude for what you've shared. Thank you, Noah.

Sincerely,

Amy

You Can't Break Universal Law

I'm often asked: "How will I know when my Afformations are working?" (This question, by the way, typically comes from people who haven't actually tried using Afformations yet!)

I've had thousands of people tell me that as soon as they started using Afformations, they felt an immediate sense of calm and peace, similar to what Amy described in her story.

They saw instant changes in their outlook on life, their emotions, and their health. And over time, they found themselves manifesting things that had once seemed impossible.

However—and this is a very important point—The Afformations Method is based on science, not magic. You cannot afform: *Why am I so thin and healthy?*, continue to eat unhealthy foods and not exercise, and expect to drop the pounds.

You can't afform: *Why is my business so successful?*, do nothing to grow your business, never do anything different than what you've done in the past, and expect it to grow—any more than you would expect a plant to grow if it were never watered or nourished.

Here's the bottom line: You cannot break the laws of the universe and expect to get the results you want. You can't continue to do negative or self-defeating actions and expect to get what you want, even if you're sitting there asking great questions! That is what's called *magical thinking,* and it's similar to believing that if you just buy enough lottery tickets and believe hard enough, you'll win the lottery. (By the way, I've interviewed more than 50 millionaires and multimillionaires, and not one of them became successful by winning the lottery. They got there by doing the work that most people won't.)

> You can't break the laws of the universe and expect to get what you want.

The point of Afformations is not to try to trick your mind, but to use it properly. You're already using Afformations anyway, but most people are doing so unconsciously, in a negative, disempowering, self-defeating way.

That's why following the four steps of The Afformations Method will enable your mind's automatic search function to produce remarkable results that are in your favor, rather than negative ones that don't benefit you or the ones you love.

Here's What I Want You to Do Now

1. Take out your list of desires that you wrote in Step One and your Afformations you wrote in Step Two. (Have I repeated this step enough?)

2. For each empowering Afformation, list three simple actions you could take to make them true. For example, if your Afformations have to do with making more money, what are three simple actions you could do *starting right now* to make more money?

If you've written Afformations for weight loss, what are three simple things you could do starting today to help you lose weight?

3. Take the actions. Yes, now I'm asking you to *do something!* Start with the first action you wrote on your list and do that one. Then go to the next one, and so on.

Remember: If nothing changes, nothing changes. Afformations aren't magic, they're science. Refer back to the D.B.A.R. Cycle that I showed you, and realize that while some results will come quickly, others will take more time. Just keep taking action and writing your results in your Afformations Journal.

4. Join the Afformations Revolution. Because you're reading this book, I'd like to personally invite you to join the Afformations Revolution. That means sharing the message of this book with as many friends, family members, and co-workers as possible in the next 48 hours. Another way to join the Afformations Revolution is to join me on our official Afformations fan page at **www.AfformationNation.com.**

You'll feel inspired by reading other people's Afformation success stories and how they used them to overcome challenges. Plus, you can share your own stories and meet other Afformers around the world—and it's free!

How to Use Part III of This Book

Part III of this book includes empowering Afformations for the Ten Major Areas of Life. Of course, no book could cover every Afformation, since the number of Afformations you can create is truly infinite.

That's why I suggest that you also use your Afformations Journal to write Afformations to suit your individual needs, in addition to the ones in this book. (Please note that some Afformations are repeated, because many fit in multiple categories.)

I've also organized each of the Ten Major Areas of Life into specific categories for ease of use. Now, when you find yourself stuck in any particular area, simply refer to the appropriate category for ideas on Afformations to help you get unstuck and produce the results you want faster, easier, and with far less effort.

Be sure to refer to our online programs, attend one of our live seminars, or join one of our exclusive mastermind programs. You can also get my free Afformations video training series at **www.NoahStJohn.com**.

• • •

And now, please enjoy your new, incredibly simple yet astonishingly empowering Afformations . . . and start reaping amazing results in your life!

• ● •

PART III

AFFORMATIONS FOR YOUR LIFE

CHAPTER 7

AFFORMATIONS ON HEALTH AND WELL-BEING

"[L]et whoever is in charge keep this simple question in her head (not, how can I always do this right thing myself? but), how can I provide for this right thing to be always done?"

— FLORENCE NIGHTINGALE

As I've mentioned, ever since I first began teaching Afformations in 1997, I've received thousands of success stories from real people around the world who've used Afformations to change their lives. Here's an amazing real-life success story from one of my readers:

> Dear Noah,
> From the time I was five years old, I was called obese. I would gain and lose weight but could never keep it off for longer than a year.

Even when I went through chemotherapy for lymphoma, I gained weight.

I work at a counseling center that deals with addictions. The head of the center told me that I was getting too obese to work there, and that I needed to address my addiction to food.

Then a friend told me about Afformations. I read everything I could about your work and started practicing it. It works!

After I read your book cover to cover, I started doing what you teach and began to *take action*. I not only stopped eating foods that weren't good for me, but I also began using Afformations just the way you teach them. And the more I kept using Afformations, the more positive and confident I became.

I am now *163 pounds lighter* than I was before I started using Afformations. Afformations even led me to go for my certification in food psychology coaching because I want to help people see that if I can do it at my age, they can, too.

I believe in your work and recommend it to everyone. Thank you so much, Noah!

Cecelia

It's true: if you don't have your health, it doesn't really matter what else you have. That's why we begin the Afformations section of this book with the subject of Health and Well-Being. It's one of the most important topics on people's minds, yet for many remains one of the most elusive goals to achieve.

Your health and well-being are determined by a number of factors:

- Your genetics
- The environment in which you were raised
- The environment you live in now
- Your lifestyle choices
- Your beliefs

There's not much you can do about the first two factors, because they were largely determined by your family of origin. However, there's plenty you can do about the last three.

> There's not much you can do about your genetics. But there's plenty you can do about your lifestyle choices.

For example, here's another inspiring story that was sent to me just the other day:

Dear Noah,

Crossing the finish line of a half marathon is always exciting, but Disney's Princess Half Marathon on February 24, 2013, was an especially sweet victory. I have been doing distance running events for years; so far, I've completed 5 full marathons and around 50 half marathons. What made this one so special? Did I have a personal best? Actually, it was my slowest time ever. It was because on February 1, 2013—just three weeks earlier—I had heart surgery.

I had signed up for this race several months before I found out I needed to have heart surgery. During several previous races, my heartbeat went wild, I couldn't breathe, and I got weak and dizzy. I even collapsed at two races. It got to a point where I was in arterial fibrillation and tachycardia for days at a time. I was so scared not knowing what was going on.

I ended up in the hospital twice. An MRI of my heart revealed damage to an artery. After an accident in 1979, I was given the wrong medication and suffered cardiac arrest, and they had to revive me. That caused the initial damage. With age and the repeated demand I put on my heart with running, the artery split. Surgery was my only option.

As I was waiting for the Princess race to start, I felt more fear than I did with my first race—or even when I had heart surgery. Even though my surgeon had encouraged me to do the race, I was really scared. What if my heart wasn't healed enough? What if I passed out again? What if I started feeling chest pain and no one was around to help me? What if I couldn't breathe again?

At that moment, I realized that I needed to do what helped me get through heart surgery: use Afformations. I began afforming: *Why is my heart so strong? Why do I feel so confident? Why do I know I will finish feeling fresh? Why do I know that I will finish one steady step after another?*

It wasn't long before I felt a surge of confidence.

Mile after mile, I repeated my Afformations. Then around mile eight, I noticed many participants begin to struggle. They asked how I could look so lively and fresh. That's when I told them about my secret weapon—Afformations.

Soon, I had a whole group of women (and one man) laughing and repeating Afformations. I watched their bodies get stronger as they experienced renewed energy. Two miles passed before we knew it!

At the ten-mile mark, I was feeling so good and so fresh that I took off running. They came up to me after the race waving their medals and thanked me for sharing such an empowering tool. At that moment, I decided to make group Afformations a new race tradition. Thank you, Noah!

Gratefully,

Cindy

I've organized the Afformations in this chapter into three categories: Physical Body, Emotional Health, and Healthy Lifestyle Choices. In the Physical Body section, rather than attempting to list every possible physical ailment a person can have, I've given you a fill-in-the-blank template that you can use to form Afformations for any physical challenge you're facing.

Then, in Emotional Health and Healthy Lifestyle Choices, I've listed Afformations to help you make better choices and get better results in these areas as well.

When you're facing a challenge in any of these areas, simply turn to this chapter to find specific Afformations you can use, and also create your own customized Afformations for your specific needs.

Use the following Afformations as a starting point to challenge your unconscious assumptions about achieving your health, fitness, or weight-loss goals; strengthen your positive beliefs; and eliminate your negative ones. Ask away!

Physical Body

- Why am I so healthy?
- Why do I love my body?
- Why am I happy when I look in the mirror?
- Why am I the perfect me?
- Why is my _____ so healthy?
- Why does my _____ work so well?
- Why is my _____ working perfectly?
- Why did my _____ heal?
- Why did my _____ get better?
- Why does my _____ work the way it should, in harmony with my body?
- Why do I have unstoppable stamina?
- Why am I so grateful that I'm so healthy?
- Why am I so lucky to have the body that I have?
- Why does everything in my body operate perfectly?
- Why am I so strong?
- Why do I have abundant energy every day?
- Why do I love my beautiful, healthy body?
- Why does my body treat me so well?

- Why did God create perfection as me?
- Why is my body a gift from God?

Emotional Health

- Why do I enjoy peace of mind and fulfillment every day?
- Why do I celebrate my health today?
- Why am I so emotionally healthy?
- Why am I so happy and comfortable in my own skin?
- Why do I see only beauty when I look in the mirror?
- Why do I attract emotionally healthy people?
- Why did I let go of the past?
- Why did I forgive _____ ?
- Why do I let go of frustration?
- Why did I let go of grief?
- Why am I so happy?
- Why do I have an open heart and create loving communication?
- Why do I release the past?
- Why am I in control of my mind, body, and spirit?

Healthy Lifestyle Choices

- Why do I take responsibility for my health?
- Why are healthy people magnetically drawn to me?
- Why do I radiate perfect health and well-being?
- Why do I eat a healthy, balanced diet?
- Why do I take such good care of myself?
- Why is it so easy for me to lose weight?
- Why do I love to exercise?
- Why do I love eating right?
- Why do I accept compliments so easily?
- Why do I treat my body with love?
- Why do my family and friends support me in my healthy lifestyle choices?
- Why did I lose my taste for foods that aren't good for me?
- Why do I take my time when I eat and really enjoy my food?
- Why do I eat a healthy balance of proteins, carbohydrates, and fats?
- Why do I make healthy choices when I prepare food for my family?
- Why do I have fun eating right and exercising?
- Why do healthy foods taste so good to me?

- Why does my body respond so well when I put healthy foods into it?

- Why does my body love eating well?

- Why do I look forward to exercising every day?

- Why does my body respond so well to healthy exercise?

- Why do I love living a healthy, active lifestyle?

- Why did I quit worrying?

- Why do I treat my body like the temple it is?

- Why do I let people support me in my new, healthy lifestyle?

- Why am I so grateful for my beautiful, healthy body?

- Why do I love living a healthy, happy life?

- Why am I emotionally, physically, financially, and spiritually healthy today and every day of my wonderful life?

• ● •

CHAPTER
8

AFFORMATIONS ON MONEY AND ABUNDANCE

*"The question isn't at what age I want to retire,
it's at what income."*

— GEORGE FOREMAN

If there's one subject where people are holding on to a ton of negative beliefs, it's in the area of Money and Abundance.

Let's start by looking at some of the common beliefs we've been told about wealth and money: "Money doesn't grow on trees," "It's easier for a camel to pass through the eye of a needle than for a rich man to enter the gates of heaven," "If you're rich, you must be selfish," "Rich people are greedy," "Rich people must have stolen from other people to make their money," and so on.

Here's what I want you to realize: your relationship with money is like your relationships with people. For example, when you treat a person poorly, he or she will not want to be around you. But when you treat someone well, they'll probably want to stick around.

Money behaves in exactly the same way. When you speak, think, or act negatively about money, it won't want to be around you. But when you speak, think, and act positively about money, it will be magnetically drawn to you.

Your relationship with money is like your relationships with people.

You might think it sounds crazy to talk about money "behaving" like a person does. However, there's one very important thing I'd like you to remember:

Money comes attached to these
strange creatures called human beings.

As I explain in my seminars and mastermind programs, money is simply a means of perceived value exchange among human beings. To paraphrase the philosopher Stuart Wilde, "The way money works is, you have some—and everyone else has all the rest."

I teach my coaching clients to think about money as a means of exchange through which you can do more good in the world. I know that you are a heart-centered, caring person who really wants to make a difference in the world. The problem is that you're probably carrying around disempowering beliefs about money that are hurting your ability to make more of it and live a more abundant lifestyle.

While it's great to want to make a difference, I want you to stop believing that it's more spiritual to be poor than to be rich. As a minister friend of mine once said, "The best way to help the poor is to not be one of them."

Don't limit your own wealth by misguidedly believing that those who have more money than you do are somehow not as "good" or "spiritual" as you are. I want you to remove the guilt and shame from your relationship with money. And yes, you do have a relationship with money, whether you have a lot or a little of it right now.

The Things We Do for Money

Think about all the things you do every day that relate to money. You perform work in exchange for it. (Can you honestly say you'd do what you do for work if you *didn't* get paid for it?) You use money to pay your bills so you have things like electricity, water, food, clothing, and shelter to help you survive. Even *worrying* about money means you're thinking about money!

Yet how many of us ever admit—even to ourselves—how much time we spend thinking about and trying to make more money?

In fact, just reading those last few paragraphs may have made you feel uncomfortable. But why? I believe much of our discomfort in talking about this subject relates to the words we use in relation to it.

Have you ever noticed that there is not one positive word in the English language to describe a person who loves money? Even the phrase "a person who loves money" feels like a negative description, doesn't it?

We think of words like *miser, hoarder, selfish,* and *greedy* when describing someone who loves money. Remember Ebenezer Scrooge from *A Christmas Carol?* No one would want to be like him, right?

Yet the fact remains that it's *not* wrong to love money. Our money problems do not occur because we love money; our money problems occur when we put money before people.

> Our money problems do not occur because we love money; they occur when we put money before people.

When you put money before people, you have the equation backward, because money is a means of perceived value exchange among people. Simply put, human beings give you money when they perceive that the *value* they're going to receive from you is greater than the amount of money they give you.

For example, I got this e-mail from Susan, a television producer from California:

Dear Noah,

When I first heard you teach Afformations and speak about your own situation, I was struck by how similar it was to my own. I have been in the entertainment industry (primarily television), as well as a student of spiritual studies, for my entire adult life. However, after a landslide destroyed our home seven years ago, I felt pulled to study coaching and schools of success philosophies, investing tens of thousands of dollars.

I devoted all my energies and funds into starting a new venture that would give me more time to work with people. Much to my dismay, by the time I heard you speak, I was failing financially. I had burned through all my savings, had no income, and was avoiding phone calls from creditors. Fortunately, my husband was willing to buy the groceries and put gasoline into the car so I could stay in any kind of activity. I was physically stuck.

It was only because your story resonated so much with me that I was willing to spend the nominal sum to purchase your Afformations System home-study program. I listened to it right away, struck by the shift of philosophy. I noted in my journal, "What if he's right? What if it *is* in the questions? It is written: ask and you will receive. What if we just have to learn how to ask?"

I followed your instructions, writing down why questions about my major problems. And then I flipped the question from a negative reinforcement of the situation into a positive suggestion for my subconscious to pursue. I could feel the difference immediately!

Then I listened to your *iAfform Audios,* and guidance began to flow, freeing my spirit to be creative.

Small bits of work began to arrive. Nothing to write home about; however, any income was a shift in a direction that lifted my spirit! I was not judging what came to me but accepting with gratitude, holding my vision, and using Afformations every day. Three months later, I had multiple job offers and took a production opportunity. And with each paycheck, my spirits lifted and my long-term vision prospered.

It's now been six months. I have finished the first draft of my book and am using it as a springboard into my program to work with others. My work is demanding, but I have been promoted and received a significant bump in salary that puts me on track as a six-figure-income earner.

What have Afformations done for me? I went from being "penniless" (no income, no savings, dependent on others for the basics of survival) to having a six-figure income in six months. I am lightening up. I am having fun. I am pursuing my greater dream. Thank you, Noah!

Many people are looking for a way to "get rich quick." The irony is that while "get rich quick" does not exist, the fastest and easiest way to become wealthy is to provide lots of value to lots of people—and keep doing it until you reach the level of income and abundance you desire.

The Afformations in this chapter are organized into two categories: Beliefs about Money and Healthy Money Habits. In the Beliefs about Money section, use these Afformations to examine your unconscious beliefs about money and how they may be holding you back. In the Healthy Money Habits section, I've listed Afformations to help you make better choices about how you use this tool called *money* in your everyday life.

Use the following Afformations to improve your relationship with money and increase your value to other people, and watch your relationships—with both money and people—become more fulfilling and more abundant every day of your new, rich life!

Beliefs about Money

- Why am I so rich?
- Why am I so wealthy?

- Why do I love being truly wealthy?

- Why am I so richly blessed?

- Why do I always have enough money?

- Why does money come to me so easily?

- Why is money no object? (Consider this question carefully. Money has no meaning in and of itself; it is simply an expression of perceived value among human beings.)

- Why do I have so much worth and value?

- Why am I worth having a positive net worth?

- Why do I have permission to be happy and wealthy?

- Why can I enjoy my wonderful wealth and still be spiritually centered?

- Why am I worthy of being wealthy?

- Why has God given me the power to be wealthy?

- Why is money such a wonderful gift to me?

- Why is money magnetically attracted to me?

- Why am I a happy money magnet?

- Why does money love being with me?

- Why is God a God of increase, abundance, and more than enough?

- Why is my life a life of increase, abundance, and more than enough?

- Why does God bless me with unprecedented favor today?

- Why do I have an abundance of money?

- Why do I love having so much money?

- Why do I enjoy being healthy, wealthy, and wise?

- Why does being rich equal being spiritual for me?

- Why do I believe and live the statement, "In God we trust"?

Healthy Money Habits

- Why does my income always exceed my expenses?

- Why do I let myself be rich and happy, too?

- Why is it okay for me to have lots of money?

- Why do I use my life of abundance to enrich the lives of others?

- Why am I happy to be so abundant?

- Why does God bless me with such financial abundance?

- Why do I invest, tithe, and spend in balance?

- Why do I love being wealthy *and* spiritual?

- Why do I no longer say things like "I'm broke" or "I can't afford it"?

- Why do I enjoy teaching my children the real value of money?

- Why do I thankfully ask and abundantly receive?

- Why is it so easy for me to express my spirituality by being financially abundant?

- Why am I grateful for all that I have?

- Why do I spend less than I earn?

- Why do I meet my financial responsibilities?

- Why do I invest my money wisely?

- Why do I find opportunities everywhere I look?

- Why does abundance find me everywhere I go?

- Why am I proud to be wealthy and happy?

- Why do I allow myself to be as wealthy as I've always wanted?

- Why don't I let anyone make me feel bad about being rich and happy?

- Why do I help those around me to be wealthier, too?

- Why do I add so much value to other people's lives—and why do I allow that to add riches to *my* life?

- Why do I love being out of debt forever?

- Why do I love being so rich and generous?

- Why am I so grateful for my life of abundance?

- Why do I thank God for my new, abundant lifestyle?

• ● •

CHAPTER 9

AFFORMATIONS ON BUILDING SELF-CONFIDENCE

*"The only questions that really matter
are the ones you ask yourself."*

— URSULA K. LE GUIN

In our live workshops and mastermind programs, we often include a fill-in-the-blank questionnaire that gets people to look at their inner beliefs about themselves.

We often ask our students to complete this phrase: "If I'm good to myself, _____." Many of the women in our workshops finish that statement by saying, "I feel guilty!"

Do you sometimes feel guilty if you take time for yourself? How do you feel accepting a sincere compliment? When someone compliments you, do you accept it, say thank you, and move on? Do you secretly wonder,

What do they want from me? Or do you wave it off, deny their compliment, and think you're being "humble"?

Listen, there's nothing wrong with a little humility. What I'm talking about is the inability to accept a sincere compliment. That happens when your Negative Reflection—that part of you that doesn't believe anything good about you—has told you lies that you believe, such as, "You're not that pretty," or "You're not good enough."

> How do you feel when someone pays you a sincere compliment?

And guess what? You believe these lies you've been telling yourself, even when someone else is trying to give you a genuine compliment. For example, I was teaching Afformations on a teleseminar, and two weeks later heard from one of the attendees. She wrote:

> Noah,
>
> Thank you for teaching us on the call. I find myself using Afformations *everywhere!* People are even asking me what I'm doing to lose weight!
>
> But the funniest part is that I haven't lost a thing! My schedule hasn't allowed me to get to the gym, and my eating hasn't changed. So the scale reads the same and I keep asking myself, "Why am I so fit and healthy at 125 pounds?"
>
> People are *seeing* what I'm *asking.* Maybe my enthusiasm is burning off those extra cheesecake calories!

Being able to accept a sincere compliment is just one behavior that reveals your beliefs about yourself and your level of self-confidence. Another is how you show up in your relationships. As an example, I've included what a student named Adam posted on our online Afformations mastermind group:

> Dear Noah,
>
> Afformations have changed my life in so many ways! Growing up, I was always an introvert and not very confident when it came to most human interactions, especially with women.
>
> After a friend told me about you and your Afformations Method, I started listening to your *iAfform Audios,* reading your books, and really working on my confidence.
>
> Right around that time, I met a woman named Samantha who was beautiful, and I thought she was out of my league. Here I was, a geeky, skinny entrepreneur just starting in business who didn't have a lot of success yet, and she had modeled a bit and was dating a very successful dentist who was also a body builder. It really intimidated me!
>
> So I started using the Afformation: *Why am I so confident?* I also started acting more confident, completely faking it at first. But I noticed that with the Afformations, the more actions I took, the more confident I really felt.
>
> Within a month, I decided to go ahead and ask her out, and it took two months for her to say yes. We are now happily married. Thank you, Noah, for helping me gain the confidence and find the relationship I always wanted!

(To learn how to join our private online Afformations mastermind group, see Part IV of this book or visit **www.HavingAbundance.com**.)

If you've been holding on to a negative self-concept or find it hard to accept a sincere compliment, use these Afformations to build a positive self-image—and let your light shine from within!

Beliefs about Yourself

- Why am I so confident?
- Why do I love feeling so confident?
- Why do I love being so confident?
- Why am I so calm?
- Why am I so capable?
- Why am I so comfortable in my own skin?
- Why did God create such beauty in and as me?
- Why am I so comfortable being Who I Really Am?
- Why am I enough?
- Why do I attract more than enough in my life?
- Why do I attract more than enough in my business?
- Why do I attract more than enough in my relationships?
- Why am I good enough, even though I'm not perfect?
- Why am I more than capable?

- Why am I perfectly equipped to do what I'm here to do?

- Why am I so loving?

- Why am I so loved?

- Why am I exactly who I'm supposed to be?

- Why is it okay to like myself?

- Why is it okay to love myself?

- Why is it okay to treat myself well?

- Why do I have *permission to succeed?*

- Why do people enjoy being around me?

- Why do I feel confident sharing my talents with the world?

- Why did God create perfection in me?

- Why am I so respected by friends, family members, and colleagues?

- Why am I so confident putting my trust in God?

- Why am I so poised?

- Why is it easy for people to get to know and like me?

- Why do people want to help me reach my goals? (Perhaps because you help them reach theirs!)

Healthy Self-Confidence Habits

- Why do I believe in myself?
- Why do I let others believe in me?
- Why do I gratefully accept every good thing that comes my way today?
- Why am I magnetically attracted to the best, most loving, and wonderful people on Earth?
- Why do I see only enoughness when I look in the mirror?
- Why do I easily see my own worth and value?
- Why do I let others see my worth and value?
- Why am I respected in my work and my life?
- Why do I accept compliments so graciously?
- Why are leaders attracted and magnetized to me?
- Why do I seek only the best in life?
- Why do I see only the best in myself and in others?
- Why do I walk away from people and situations that aren't good for me?
- Why do I enjoy sharing my gifts with the world?
- Why am I always in the right place at the right time doing the right thing with the right people?
- Why do I attract loving, healthy people?
- Why do I let go of negative people?

- Why do people value and appreciate me?
- Why am I so great at seizing opportunities?
- Why am I allowed to be all I really want in this life?
- Why am I allowed to do all I really want in this life?
- Why am I allowed to have all I really want in this life?
- Why do I always come from love?
- Why do I always come from more than enough?
- Why do I come from a place of contributing to the lives of others?
- Why do I love making people feel good about themselves today?
- Why do I look for the best in others?
- Why do I love catching people doing things right?
- Why am I so good at seizing opportunities today?
- Why am I so grateful that I'm so confident?
- Why has God blessed me so much today and every day of my life?

● ● ●

AFFORMATIONS ON WORK AND CAREER

"Einstein was a man who could ask immensely simple questions. And what his life showed, and his work, is that when the answers are simple too, then you hear God thinking."

— JACOB BRONOWSKI

George, a client from Texas, sent me the following story:

Dear Noah,
Using Afformations the way you teach them has changed my life—it's like night and day.

My life is drastically different from the day I started writing my Afformations to today, in every aspect: spiritually (better connected, more peace), family life (got married), financial (an increase of over *ten times* what I was making before), nutrition and fitness (eating nutritiously and working out), planning out my family's future and security, and *way* less stress because of the improvements in all areas of my life.

When I started writing my goals, I was in a pretty bad spot. Finances were tight, my business was far from successful, and I thought my time had come and gone. My family life was also a mess.

The financial results are the most impressive, of course, and probably what most people can relate to: I have people seeking me out that I don't even know, and after the first phone calls, I got checks for between $5,000 and $10,000 on their way to me (and these are monthly clients), and this happens several times a month.

I'll be honest—some days early on I was writing and thinking about my Afformations, and I felt like things were never going to change. Eventually, they gave me laser focus, and I just drilled it in my brain that I deserve more out of life.

Most of us are on autopilot when we go on about our day, and we're not focusing on what we want out of life (as in, our goals and how we want our lives to turn out).

Also, using Afformations opened my eyes to new opportunities that I never saw before. It's not that the opportunities weren't there or never headed my way; it's that I didn't have my antenna up to receive them.

This isn't magic or hocus-pocus. It's what happens when you know what you want out of life and remind yourself consistently. Before you know it, you will be overwhelmed with ideas and opportunities.

Noah, I am recommending you to all my friends and telling them, "If you're not happy with the direction your life is headed in—or you just want *more*—you need to check out Noah's trainings. As long as you start applying what he teaches you, and remain consistent, you will see improvements."

Sometimes people say, "Oh, you're into that law of attraction stuff," and they sort of write it off as magic or hocus-pocus. But I tell them it's not that at all; you're just turning on your antenna to find the best pathway to reach your goals because you're now aware of what you want out of life.

So if you want to call it magic—then it's about as magic as turning on a radio!

Thank you, Noah. You rock!

Another client sent me the following story:

Dear Noah,

I wanted to share my story with you about my first experience with Afformations.

I was very dissatisfied with my job. Many were the days I would come to work and ask myself why I still came. I found no fulfillment in what I did—and the pay, which never has been very stellar, was becoming less and less desirable.

Looking for change at work as well as for answers as to why I had failed at three different business ventures in the past two and a half years, I bought your online Afformations System program and started studying your material.

After hearing you teach Afformations and reading about them in your books, I decided to turn around the questions I was asking myself. Instead of asking myself why I wasn't happy at work and why I didn't find fulfillment there, I started asking myself, *Why do I enjoy my work so much?* and *Why is work so fulfilling for me?*

In all honesty, I wasn't really diligent in asking myself these questions. But whenever I found myself starting to think negatively about my job or caught myself asking why I didn't like it, I would quickly turn to my Afformation questions and ask them several times instead.

In early December, the CEO of my company was looking for someone to take on several new projects that needed to be done. I looked at my role within the company—my job duties, skills, and abilities. I then compared that with the skills needed to do the projects. I suddenly realized that I was the one that should be doing those projects!

Taking this new thinking into consideration, I used my Afformations more frequently. I started asking myself those new questions without even knowing that there could, or would, be a new role for me.

About a week and a half later, I found the perfect opportunity to approach the CEO about those projects. I told him that I thought the company needed to hire someone to take on those projects, and that the person they should hire was me!

I even found the courage to tell him that I was dissatisfied with the way my pay had been negotiated the last time I had been given a new assignment at work, and I deserved something more if I took on this new role.

Well, within a week the deal was done. The CEO created a new position in the company and approached me about the new compensation he would be willing to pay. I now had a new job with more than twice the pay!

At first I didn't even realize that what I had been doing with the Afformations was connected to what had just happened. But as I've been looking over your home-study materials again, it finally hit me. I had significantly altered the way I was interpreting the world because of what you taught me.

I had gone from seeing my world negatively and asking why it was so, to asking myself why I was so blessed and work was so wonderful. Just as you teach, because I had been asking negative questions, the world was responding with negative results.

Once I changed what I was asking for, the world produced something completely different!

I know that I went through your home-study materials much too fast the first time. But thank heavens the Afformations had the impact they did!

Thank you,
Michael

P.S. I am on my way through your Afformations System course a second time and am looking forward to getting even more out of it this
time around!

Do you hate your job? If so, it's time to ask yourself
some tough questions. Here are a few:

- What is causing me to feel this way?
- What can I do about it?
- Who can help me change this result?

If you hate your job, it's probably for a specific reason: because there's something else you'd rather be
doing with your time. The problem is that
most people don't know what the
"something else" is.

> If you hate your job, it's time to ask your-self some tough questions.

We spend most of our waking
lives at work. Therefore, if you hate
your job, you are spending the greatest amount of your waking life doing
something you don't like—and that's
not the road to an abundant lifestyle.

Yes, these are challenging times. And challenging
times call for new thoughts, new beliefs, and especially new actions. The great news is that you are far more
powerful, are far more capable, and have far more ability
than you know.

That's why I encourage you to start asking yourself
new questions about your own skills, talents, and abilities and the world around you—and get ready to see a
brand-new you springing forth!

Beliefs about Work

- Why am I so successful?

- Why am I so confident in my work?

- Why do I love my job?

- Why can I get what I want?

- Why is my work so satisfying to me?

- Why am I so lucky to be doing the work I do?

- Why do I love expressing Who I Really Am—and being fabulously well-paid for doing it?

- Why am I so valuable to people?

- Why do I love what I do?

- Why is my work fulfilling for me?

- Why do I have the courage to do what I love and ask for the money I'm worth?

- Why do opportunities come to me so easily and so often?

- Why am I fundamentally unstoppable?

- Why is it okay for me to be as successful as I really want to be?

- Why do I feel comfortable being very successful?

- Why do I attract the right mentors and people to help me on my career path?

- Why am I validated at work and at home?

- Why are my talents expressed and appreciated at work?

- Why are my natural gifts recognized and well compensated?

- Why are my goals coming to me as fast as I'm coming to them?

- Why am I so clear about my vision for success?

- Why am I so comfortable being so successful in life and business?

- Why does success find me everywhere I go?

- Why am I proud to be happy and successful?

- Why do I thank God for my success?

- Why do I let myself be as successful as I like?

- Why does success come to me so quickly and so easily now?

- Why does being successful equal being spiritual for me?

Healthy Work Habits

- Why do I take full advantage of every opportunity that comes my way?

- Why do I have more than enough?

- Why does having what I want help others get what they want?

- Why do I visualize my plan so vividly?
- Why do I follow through on my plans?
- Why am I at peace with success?
- Why did I stop stopping myself from success?
- Why is my career growing beyond my wildest dreams?
- Why do I love what I do and do what I love?
- Why do I always act with integrity?
- Why do I give myself *permission to succeed?*
- Why am I secure in my work?
- Why do I love to win?
- Why do I feel comfortable asking for the sale?
- Why am I so appreciated for the work I do?
- Why do I allow myself to be more successful than I ever dreamed?
- Why do I let myself live the life of my dreams?
- Why do I have so much success in business?
- Why do I love being truly happy and successful?
- Why do I love being healthy, wealthy, and wise?
- Why do I love helping people and making healthy profits at the same time?
- Why does my business bring in more than it spends?

- Why do successful people love being around me?

- Why is it so easy for me to change when change is necessary?

- Why do I help those around me to be more successful?

- Why do I lead by example?

- Why do I enjoy adding so much value to other people's lives?

- Why do I thank God for the successful life I now live, every day of my blessed life?

• ● •

CHAPTER 11

AFFORMATIONS ON LOVE AND INTIMACY

*"If love is the answer, could you
please rephrase the question?"*

— LILY TOMLIN

During one of our live seminars in Denver, something happened to a young woman in our audience. She was attractive, intelligent, and caring, so I noticed that people were naturally drawn to her.

Yet when I asked her to answer questions about her opinion of herself and her worth in relationships, she burst into tears! After having gone through a devastating divorce and other unsuccessful relationships, her thoughts for future love were almost hopeless.

After she learned about Afformations, she realized she was unknowingly asking disempowering questions like: *Why do I keep failing at love? Why does love hurt so much? Why am I unlovable? Why haven't I found the man of my dreams?* and *Why am I not worthy of the love I desire?*

What do you think her life looked like? Exactly: her life had become the literal embodiment of her disempowering Afformations. Her subconscious questions had formed a life where she had no confidence in her ability to love and be loved. She began to think that maybe there was no such thing as true, lasting love. It was the definition of a self-fulfilling prophecy.

Less than 90 days after the seminar, she called our offices, so excited she could hardly breathe! After she caught her breath, she told me that my seminar had been the turning point in her life—because for the first time, she saw that she was asking the wrong questions, and they were ruining her life.

Once she understood the true power of Afformations, she immediately stopped asking disempowering questions and began using a single empowering Afformation that changed her life: *Why do I have the most incredibly loving relationship with the man of my dreams?*

As this woman started asking her new Afformation, her mind's automatic search function began to form new patterns. She started to see things differently. She realized that she'd been stopping herself from being loved because of the negative, disempowering questions she'd been unknowingly asking herself.

The Afformation she began using was, *Why do I have the most incredibly loving relationship with the man of my dreams?*

She decided to take a leap of faith. Then she took *action!* Her new Afformation allowed her to open her mind and heart to the possibility of true love.

She took a risk, opened her heart to love again, and met the man she eventually married—all because she dared to ask herself a new question and take action!

The Three Phases of Love

There are three distinct phases of love: your inner beliefs about love; the process of finding the right person for you; and maintaining a healthy, intimate relationship with your significant other. If you are holding on to disempowering beliefs in any of these phases, your intimate relationships will inevitably suffer.

For example, let's say you're holding on to disempowering beliefs about love, like the young woman in my seminar. If this is the case, it's going to be very hard for you to find the right person for you until you change those beliefs.

Or, what if you unconsciously believe that you can't be in a happy, long-term relationship with another person? If this is true, then even if you do find the right person for you, you'll probably find ways to sabotage the relationship—even though you won't realize why you're doing it.

I've given you empowering Afformations for each phase of love, because I want you to find the happiness and love you deserve in relationships. Yes, it's true: love makes everything better. But its absence can make life seem awfully empty.

How to Find Love Right Where You Are

If you find yourself looking for love in all the wrong places, the reason is because you are asking the wrong questions, holding on to the wrong beliefs, or taking the wrong actions (or none at all). Conversely, if you're unhappy in your relationship with your significant other, you're unknowingly asking disempowering Afformations that are causing you to focus on the negative rather than the positive—and on what you *can't* do and *don't* have, rather than what you *can* do and *do* have.

As I've said throughout this book, and as the greatest teachers in history have taught us, what we focus on grows. Use these Afformations on love to refocus your mind on the gifts of love that you *have,* and the gift of love that you *are.*

Beliefs about Love

- Why am I so loved?
- Why am I so loving?
- Why do I enjoy happy, healthy, peaceful relationships?
- Why is my love life so fulfilling?
- Why is it easy for me to ask for the love I really want?
- Why do I easily accept the love I really need?
- Why do I let myself love unconditionally?
- Why am I willing to give love a second chance?

- Why do I let myself be open to love?

- Why am I safe to love and be loved?

- Why do I love purely?

- Why do I have such passion?

- Why do loving, happy people love being around me?

- Why are my relationships so much fun?

- Why am I safe to love again?

- Why do I easily accept love in my life?

- Why does being loved equal being spiritual for me?

- Why is it so easy for me to express the love I really feel?

- Why are my relationships so loving, fun, and healthy?

- Why am I an expression of God's love here on Earth?

- Why is my life totally filled with love?

- Why is love Who I Really Am?

Attracting the Right Partner

- Why is it so easy to find the person of my dreams?

- Why am I so grateful to find the perfect person for me?

- Why is it so easy for me to find love again?

- Why am I open to love again?

- Why am I so supportive of my significant other?

- Why does God want me to find true love?

- Why are my relationships precious gifts from God?

- Why do I forgive and let go of the past?

- Why does my past not equal my future?

- Why do I have the courage to love again?

- Why do I easily let love in?

- Why am I loved for being Who I Really Am?

- Why is it so easy for me to find my soul mate?

- Why did love come to me so quickly and easily now?

- Why do I love being so attractive to the person I truly want to meet?

- Why is it so easy for me to be happy, loved, and loving?

- Why do I create an atmosphere of love in my life?

- Why do I attract happy, healthy relationships?

Healthy Love Habits

- Why do I respect my significant other?

- Why do I appreciate all my partner is and does?

- Why is love so easy for me?

- Why do I catch my significant other doing something right every day?

- Why do I have a sense of humor in dealing with the people in my life?

- Why do I not expect my partner to be perfect?

- Why do I fall in love with my significant other every day?

- Why do I love and forgive those around me?

- Why do I have so much love in my life?

- Why am I so grateful that I'm so loved?

- Why am I so comfortable giving and receiving love and intimacy?

- Why do I seek to understand my partner before I assume?

- Why do I give love and allow myself to receive love?

- Why do I love having healthy intimacy?

- Why is it so easy for me to truly listen and be in the moment with my partner?

- Why do I live a truly loving life today and every day?

- Why do I give love wisely?

- Why do I receive love openly?

- Why do I find so many fun and simple ways to give and receive love today?

- Why am I emotionally committed to being with my partner?

- Why am I proud to be the loving person I really am?

- Why do I allow myself to be as loved as I've always wanted?

- Why do I give and receive love in just the right ways?

- Why do I help those around me to feel more loved, too?

- Why do I love being so loving and generous?

- Why are my actions those of a truly happy, loving person?

- Why do I thank God for all the love I have, today and every day of my life?

• ● •

AFFORMATIONS ON FAMILY AND RELATIONSHIPS

"Life's most persistent and urgent question is, What are you doing for others?"

— MARTIN LUTHER KING, JR.

One of my first coaching clients was a home-based business owner named Barbara. Barbara was smart, hardworking, and had great people skills—but felt frustrated because she was holding herself back from the success she knew she was capable of. A friend told her about our **SuccessClinic.com** website, and she contacted me and asked me to coach her to break through her old barriers.

As we worked together through my transformational coaching method, Barbara started working through her fears of success. I suggested she write Afformations related to the outcome she wanted, like being more successful in business. She realized that she wanted her husband to be more supportive of her work, so one of the Afformations she wrote was, *Why is my husband so supportive of me and my success?*

On our coaching call the very next week, she told me, "Noah, it's like a miracle!"

As she was getting ready for work and her husband was downstairs—doing the same routine they'd been doing for 20 years—she was afforming to herself her new, positive questions. Suddenly, something happened that had never happened in 20 years of marriage: her husband called up the stairs and said, "Have a great day, honey. I love you!"

> She called the very next week and said: "Noah, it's like a miracle!"

Then, later in the day, her husband called her after one of her sales meetings and asked, "How did your meeting go?" He had never done that before either!

She went on to have the best year of her career. Afformations not only improved her marriage, but they also helped her increase her self-confidence and grow her business.

How to Have Happy Relationships

Every human being you will ever meet is wearing two invisible signs. The first sign says: PLEASE MAKE ME FEEL IMPORTANT. The second one says: HELP ME FIRST.

That means all people are waiting for someone to make them feel important and to help them get the things they want. The problem is that everyone is waiting for *everyone else* to go first!

That's why I encourage my coaching clients to be the ones who go first. The more you acknowledge, appreciate, and seek to help others—not from a position of "they're better than me," but from a position of "I have so much to give"—the more people will be magnetically drawn to you.

An ancient parable often told by Rabbi Haim of Romshishok illustrates this principle:

I once ascended to the firmaments. I first went to see Hell and the sight was horrifying. Row after row of tables were laden with platters of sumptuous food, yet the people seated around the tables were pale and emaciated, moaning in hunger. As I came closer, I understood their predicament.

Every person held a full spoon, but both arms were splinted with wooden slats so he could not bend either elbow to bring the food to his mouth. It broke my heart to hear the tortured groans of these poor people as they held their food so near but could not consume it.

Next I went to visit Heaven. I was surprised to see the same setting I had witnessed in Hell—row after row of long tables laden with food. But in contrast to Hell, the people here in Heaven were sitting contentedly talking with each other, obviously sated from their sumptuous meal.

As I came closer, I was amazed to discover that here, too, each person had his arms splinted on wooden slats that prevented him from bending his elbows. How, then, did they manage to eat?

As I watched, a man picked up his spoon and dug it into the dish before him. Then he stretched across the table and fed the person across from him! The recipient of this kindness thanked him and returned the favor by leaning across the table to feed his benefactor.

I suddenly understood. Heaven and Hell offer the same circumstances and conditions. The critical difference is in *the way the people treat each other* [emphasis mine].

I ran back to Hell to share this solution with the poor souls trapped there. I whispered in the ear of one starving man, "You do not have to go hungry. Use your spoon to feed your neighbor, and he will surely return the favor and feed you."

"You expect me to feed the detestable man sitting across the table?" said the man angrily. "I would rather starve than give him the pleasure of eating!"

I then understood God's wisdom in choosing who is worthy to go to Heaven and who deserves to go to Hell.

From Moshe Kranc,
"Heaven or Hell: A Corporate Parable,"
www.hodu.com/parable.shtml

The moral of this parable is that any one of us can make a heaven of hell and a hell of heaven. The difference lies in your answer to Dr. King's question that opened this chapter: "What are you doing for others?"

As this book was going to press, I received the following story from one of my coaching clients. I told my publisher that this story was so moving and inspiring that we had to "stop the presses" so I could share it with you here:

Dear Noah,

My father became very ill early in 2009. My parents still lived in the Toronto area, about a five-hour drive between us. Things got beyond my Mom's ability to handle, and soon I was heading back home every weekend or two. What we thought was Alzheimer's turned out to be brain cancer. We lost my father on Father's Day 2009.

My parents independently moved to Canada from Germany, and our family was pretty much our own, with little in terms of a support network. We did not have aunts, uncles, cousins, or grandparents in the area. By extension, many family functions, including funerals and weddings, were not as familiar as they were to others.

The eulogy was on my shoulders, as were many of the funeral arrangements. This was something I was not prepared for. We had about a week before what was announced for the memorial service.

I was getting a picture slide show assembled. This was pretty easy. Dig through albums, scan and organize the images in a logical order. It was kind of neat to go through the old snapshots in various evolutions of photography—black and white, early color, Polaroids, slides, and finally digital images.

But what to say? I simply did not know how to proceed.

I started to write a script and a eulogy. But I could not. It just came through in fragments, a mess. This went on for a day or so, in what was a short week and a half. I had no idea what to do.

Here is where Afformations performed miracles.

As Noah's classes guided, I scribbled down, *Why am I going to honor my father's passing in a meaningful and inspirational way?* It was all I could come up with. At that point, I was spent and went to bed.

The next day, Wednesday, there were a few more calls and administrative functions. That was as close as I came to functional. Still no inspiration on the words needed for a rapidly approaching Sunday memorial. I rewrote the Afformation, as I had done before, on a small piece of paper. *Deep breath, write something, anything.* A few bullet points and a fragmented paragraph took hours. At least it was a start.

I rewrote the Afformation on another piece of paper. I could do no more that day.

Thursday, I tried again. Afformation first. Rewrite of prior day's efforts. More words came, a story came, a theme emerged. God, this was tough. How the heck was I was going to hold it together in front a roomful of friends and family?

Then, another breakthrough arrived. I realized that this was a celebration of a life well lived. *Smile, enjoy this.* Form the words, project the feeling. Smile, even though that was the last thing that felt right. Smile and focus on the words.

Amazingly, during the reading in my small home office, it worked. I could do this.

Friday morning. Re-afform. Another rewrite. This was coming together.

Saturday was a blur.

Sunday. Time was short. Memorial slideshow looked great. Re-afform. Now I needed to do another quiet read through of the eulogy. Man, it was tough—details to add, points to clarify. *Stay calm, this will work out.*

Sunday afternoon. People arrived, tears were shed, laughs were shared. The memorial started. Pieces fell into place. Time to speak.

The Afformation came back to me. I smiled and started. It turned out right. It was natural, heartfelt, and wonderful. It all worked out.

As tough as it was, I cannot imagine how I would have done it without Afformations.

Thank you, Noah.

If you'd like to improve your relationships—whether on the job, in the home, or with your family—use the Afformations that follow, and I'll bet you'll see miracles come true for you, too.

Beliefs about Relationships

- Why am I so happy in my relationships?

- Why do I have so many wonderful friends?

- Why do I have so many happy, healthy relationships?

- Why are the happiest people on Earth attracted to me?

- Why can I count on my friends to be there when I need them?

- Why am I there for my friends when they need me?

- Why are people so generous with me?

- Why am I so generous with others?

- Why are such great people magnetically attracted to me?

- Why is my family so loving?

- Why am I so lucky in relationships?

- Why are my relationships a reflection of God's Love?

- Why am I good enough to have so many great and healthy relationships?

- Why do the people in my life recognize my strengths, talents, and abilities?

- Why do I love being happy in my relationships?

- Why do I attract happy, loving people?

- Why am I truly happy and whole?

- Why do I love being happy and whole?

- Why do happy, healthy people love being around me?

- Why do happy people find me everywhere I go?

- Why am I proud to be happy and healthy?

- Why do I let myself be as happy as I've always wanted?

Healthy Relationship Habits

- Why do people see the wonderful person I really am?

- Why do my friends tell me the truth about me?

- Why do I have so many Loving Mirrors? (As I teach in my seminars and coaching programs, a Loving Mirror is someone who sees you for Who You Really Are and supports you in living your dreams. Visit **www.NoahStJohn.com** to connect with other Afformers and Loving Mirrors around the world.)

- Why am I a Loving Mirror to my friends and family?

- Why do I actively look for the good in people?

- Why is it so easy for me to acknowledge the good I see in others?

- Why do I find something to like in everyone I meet?

- Why am I supportive of the people in my life?

- Why do I support my friends unconditionally?

- Why do my friends offer their support to me?

- Why do I enjoy rich relationships with wonderful people?

- Why do I have such a strong support network?

- Why do I forgive the past?

- Why do I take full responsibility for my life?

- Why do I enrich the lives of everyone I meet?

- Why do I recognize the greatness in each of my children and let them know they make a difference?

- Why do I lead my children by example?

- Why do I support other people's efforts to change and grow?

- Why do I let myself be happier than I ever dreamed?

- Why do I design a lifestyle of abundance?

- Why do I let myself enjoy the relationships of my dreams?

- Why do I have so much happiness in my relationships?

- Why do I like the people in my life?

- Why do I love having such healthy relationships?

- Why do I invest my energy in people wisely?

- Why do I find creative and fun ways to add value to people's lives?

- Why do I mirror the best in others?

- Why do I lead by example?

- Why do I love having lots of healthy relationships?

- Why do I love being so happy and generous?

- Why do I love having so many great friends?

- Why do I thank God for all of my happiness and joy, every day of my beautiful life?

• ● •

CHAPTER 13

AFFORMATIONS ON CONQUERING FEAR

*"Fear is a question: What are you afraid of,
and why? [O]ur fears are a treasure house
of self-knowledge if we explore them."*

— MARILYN FERGUSON

Do you know what fear is? Well, here's what it *isn't*. Fear is *not* False Evidence Appearing Real. Yes, I know you've heard that cliché a thousand times before—and you were expecting me to say it again, weren't you?

The truth is, years ago, some clever speaker came up with that acronym; unfortunately, it's become one of the most widely accepted clichés in our industry. In fact, we've heard it so many times that we've come to accept it as truth. But that's *not* what fear really is.

Here's what fear really is: *the anticipation of pain*. Fear is a very real human emotion that occurs when you anticipate or expect that something may hurt you. When you feel the emotion of fear, you're essentially saying to yourself, "Hey! What if doing _____ causes me pain?" Ironically, the emotion of fear is there to protect you; but it can also hold you back from being the person you were meant to be.

We experience the feeling of fear when we perceive that we're not in control. Fear is the emotional effect of the perceived absence of personal control. Therefore, there's an inverse relationship between control and fear. The more control we have over our lives, the less fear we feel.

> The more control we have over our lives, the less fear we feel.

The Most Basic Human Fear and How to Overcome It

The most basic human fear is the fear of rejection: "What if I do this and that person rejects me?" Why is this the most basic human fear? Centuries ago, we humans lived in tribes as a means of survival. And if we did something bad, it was deemed a crime against the tribe. In those cultures, the worst punishment was not death, but banishment from the tribe—because if you were banished, there was virtually no chance you would survive out there on your own.

How does this relate to the fear of rejection in our modern society? It shows up all the time—in social settings, in business, at home, and in our family life. Let's say you're a salesperson, and you want to increase your sales. What's one of the best ways to do that? Call your current customers and see if they want to buy something else from you.

You've probably had the thought to do this many times. But what do average salespeople do? Their very next thought is, *Oh, I don't want to bother them; they probably wouldn't be interested anyway.*

The average person knows what to do but doesn't do it, because he or she gives in to the fear of rejection. But look at what highly successful people do. Even if they feel that fear of rejection and hear that thought in their minds, they pick up the phone and start calling anyway! That's why one of the main differences between highly successful individuals and those who are average is that highly successful people feel the fear and take action anyway.

How can you develop the habit of taking action in the face of fear? Since fear is the anticipation of pain, one of the fastest ways to release any fear is to *accept the pain that you might feel as a result of taking action.* For example, in my younger days, I didn't have a fear of rejection—I had the *certainty* of rejection! When you grow up as a scrawny, geeky kid with Coke-bottle glasses and shoulder-width hair, it's not hard to see why I was painfully shy and afraid to talk to strangers.

I finally came to understand that almost everyone has the same fear of rejection that I had. Then I started doing a mental exercise, where I would imagine the person I was talking to rejecting me and then imagine how I would feel afterward.

Guess what? Once I emotionally accepted the pain of being rejected by a total stranger—someone who didn't know me anyway—I actually felt more in control of the situation, since I realized that it wasn't going to hurt me as badly as I feared it would.

Developing this habit gave me more confidence to be myself with everyone I met. It even gave me enough confidence to call a gorgeous blonde I met one day and ask her to go dancing with me—and she eventually became my wife!

In another example, Scott posted the following story on our online Afformations mastermind group:

> Dear Noah:
>
> Woo hoo! My business is on pace to *double* this month. I am using your *Ultimate Business Success iAfform Audio,* and it's awesome. I let it run on my laptop when going to sleep, so as to bypass the conscious (critical) mind. Prior to finding Afformations, I tried several home-based businesses, but my own limiting programming created a self-imposed barrier. I called it "fear of rejection," when it was really the fear of success.
>
> Simply put, I didn't think I deserved to succeed, so I was actually repelling positive results. Only about five weeks after starting Afformations, I have identified two serious business builders, and one of them has already enrolled their first customer. This is more than I accomplished with any other business effort in the last decade. Thank you!

Just the other day, I received this inspiring story of how Afformations helped a talented artist overcome her fears:

> Dear Noah,
>
> I wanted to write to you to tell you how Afformations have changed my life and led me back to my passion and purpose.
>
> I have been a professional singer/songwriter and workshop leader for most of my adult life. I

always felt that music was my calling, but after recovering from a long illness, I was afraid I wouldn't make enough money with my music to cover my enormous medical bills. Out of fear, I decided to take a full-time job as an office manager in an orthodontic practice.

I threw myself heart and soul into my job, spending long hours attending to everything I was tasked with. I would come home exhausted each night, and my music took a backseat. I would sing and write songs all the way to work and then force myself to focus on my job—convincing myself that this was they only way I could pay my bills. I struggled to find the energy to write and perform on weekends; but when I did, I felt totally in my element and so happy!

When anyone found out that I was working in a dental office during the day, they would give me a puzzled look and say, "What in the world are you doing working in a dental office when it is so obvious that your gift is music?" And I secretly wondered the same thing.

Then I attended your seminar and heard you speak about Afformations. When you explained how to use Afformations to realize your dreams, I had one of the biggest "Aha!" moments of my life!

You revealed to me the missing piece I had been searching for. Would such a simple and easy process really make a difference?

I went home and asked myself this question: *Why am I singing and songwriting as my full-time career?*

Tears filled my eyes, and I felt a lump in my throat as my answer came swiftly and sweetly: *Because I am not afraid anymore.*

I started asking empowering questions just like you taught us, and the answers flooded my thoughts and dreams. Thoughts grew into actions. And things began to change.

I started to see more bookings for my music come in. I began working fewer hours at the orthodontic office and devoted more time to writing and singing. I could feel myself being gently pulled toward my dream.

Clients started asking me to expand my services and speak at their events or lead workshops. Soon my day job dissolved before my eyes, because I felt no need to hold on anymore as the fear was replaced with courage.

I saw myself step out and trust. My heartfelt wish to make a difference in the world with my music was realized as children from India embraced the songs I wrote for the Girls for the World program, and survivors and caregivers of those with cancer felt the healing message in the songs I wrote and performed for the Relay for Life.

Today, more than ever, I am filled with passion and purpose. My heart is wide open, and I love what I do. As I move forward, I will continue to use Afformations, because I know they work!

Thank you, Noah, for Afformations—they led me back to my purpose!

Am I saying that when you use Afformations, you'll never feel fear again? No. What I am saying, however, is that using Afformations, if you use them properly, will help you *take action in the face of fear.* There's no denying that it's perfectly natural to feel hurt when someone disapproves of you or rejects you, and also totally normal to feel fear when you're thinking of trying something new.

Use the following Afformations to find the courage to do that thing you're afraid of and take that action to express more of Who You Really Are—because on the other side of your fear lies the freedom you desire.

Beliefs about Life

- Why am I enough?
- Why am I safe?
- Why did everything work out better than I thought it would?
- Why am I going to be okay?
- Why is God right here with me?
- Why am I free from worry?
- Why am I so calm?
- Why am I at peace?
- Why is it so easy for me to find solutions to challenges I face?
- Why am I so confident?
- Why am I so relaxed?

- Why am I more than capable enough to handle this?

- Why do I feel peace?

- Why does God take great care of me?

- Why am I so peaceful?

- Why does peace manifest in my life?

- Why am I greater than my fears?

- Why is there no fear with God?

- Why do people see the wonderful person I really am?

- Why am I loved so easily and so much?

- Why are people so friendly and helpful to me?

- Why do so many great people love and support me?

Feeling Safe

- Why is loneliness an illusion?

- Why is every day filled with pleasure and peace?

- Why do I easily and gratefully let go of past hurts?

- Why do I let myself win today?

- Why do I let go of irrational beliefs and let myself be happy?

- Why do I allow God to fill my life with calm?

- Why am I strong enough in mind, body, and soul to do anything I choose?

- Why am I fundamentally unstoppable?

- Why do I have the power of God within me?

- Why do I forgive and let go so easily?

- Why do I know everything will turn out great?

- Why am I safe to _____ (fill in with whatever you fear: speak in public, look for a job, enjoy healthy relationships, succeed)?

- Why did everything work out for the highest good of all concerned?

- Why am I so grateful to share my talents with the world?

- Why do I love making phone calls to great people?

- Why do I get to serve others through my products/services/ideas?

- Why is "lack" not real?

- Why am I completely protected by God?

- Why do I lovingly accept my new, true self?

- Why do I give myself permission to be Who I Really Am?

- Why am I safe to do the things I really want to do?

- Why am I safe to succeed in whatever I set my mind to?

- Why do I love being and expressing Who I Really Am?

- Why do I love my new, healthy habits?

- Why do I let myself be Who I Really Am?

- Why do I love being good at what I do?

- Why am I free from the past?

- Why do I love my new, confident self?

- Why does F.E.A.R. now stand for *Feel Everything And Relax?*

• ● •

AFFORMATIONS ON OVERCOMING BAD HABITS

For every question, there is an answer. Where everybody fails is by asking the wrong question.

— RICHARD DIAZ

What are habits and what makes them "good" or "bad"? Simply put, a habit is something you do repeatedly, usually without thinking about it. If you were to list your normal, everyday habits (for example, your daily routine), it would probably look something like this:

- Wake up in the morning
- Bathe
- Get ready for work
- Eat breakfast
- Travel to work

- Work
- Eat lunch
- Work some more
- Come home
- Eat dinner
- Go to bed at night

Sounds like a typical day, doesn't it? And these are perfectly normal habits, right? The problem is that it's not so much *what* we do as *how* we do it that creates either an abundant lifestyle or an unhappy one. That's why I'd like you to look at *how* you are doing things as well as *what* you are actually doing.

For example, let's look at the very first thing most people do in the morning: get up and get ready to go to work. How are you performing that simple act? Are you doing it grudgingly or gratefully? Happily or heavily? With agitation or with ease?

Does the conversation in your head sound something like this:

Another day, another dollar . . .

>*Back to the ol' grind . . .*

>*$#*&ing office . . .*

> Or is it: *Gosh, I love my job!* (Hey, stop laughing!)

> It's more important to look at *how* you are going through your day than *what* you are actually doing.

Next you find yourself at work and, uh, working. The question is: *How* are you performing your duties at work? Are you procrastinating on that big project, saying, "That's not my job" and hoping someone else does it, miserably doing the least you possibly can and watching every minute on the clock tick by until day's end? (Yes, I did all of these when I was working at jobs I hated!)

Or are you going through your daily checklist and getting things done as needed, asking for support and guidance when you need help, and looking for how you can add the most value to other people throughout your day?

If you're doing things from the preceding paragraph, can you see how your day is going to be vastly different than if you're doing things from the one before it?

Now let's say you're coming home after a day's work. Do you:

- Stay at the office as long as possible to avoid what you think you'll come home to

- Call home and say, "Sorry, honey, it's gonna be another late night . . ."

- Take a detour to your local watering hole to drown the day's sorrows

Or do you:

- Leave the office at a reasonable hour

- Arrive home with a sense of peace, knowing you did a good day's work

- Get a good night's sleep, knowing you're doing what you're here on Earth to do

It's pretty clear which camp we want to be in. So how do we get there?

The Three Kinds of Habits, and How to Master Them

There are three kinds of habits:

1. Habits of Thought
2. Habits of Word
3. Habits of Action

In your life, your *actions* stem from your *words,* which come from your *thoughts,* which are your *beliefs.* That means your thoughts (beliefs) create your words, which create your actions, which create your results, which create your life.

The fascinating thing about your thoughts, as we've seen in this book, is that you have two levels of thought—conscious and subconscious. That's why you might think you're having one kind of thought, when in reality—and unbeknownst to you—you're really having another. No wonder it can be so hard to overcome your Belief Gap!

Disempowering thoughts lead to habits we normally call "bad." These are habits like procrastination, smoking, biting your fingernails, gritting your teeth, overeating, overspending, gossiping at work, lashing out in anger, and so forth. Taken to an extreme, bad habits can lead to addictions such as gambling, drugs, and worse.

Addiction is the soul's way of hiding from itself.

When we look at habits in this way, we see that negative ones are caused by disempowering beliefs such as, *Why does nothing ever work out for me?* or even the most disempowering thought in human history: *Why me?*

Seen in this light, bad habits are actually a way to avoid feeling pain (for example, the pain of rejection, failure, loneliness, boredom, and so on). Bad habits and addictions, therefore, are the soul's way of hiding from itself.

An anonymous reader sent me the following story:

> Noah,
>
> I saw your interview on TV and requested that the station have you on again!
>
> I must also tell you that several weeks ago I spoke about your book and the wisdom it provides to about 25 people in my company division.
>
> Today I saw some of those same people, and they are using Afformations. One of them even told me that I saved his life by telling him about your book.
>
> He quit smoking five weeks ago and credits your book as the reason why. Now every time he gets the urge he asks himself, *Why did I quit smoking?*
>
> He always gets the answers to support his decision, and thus fends off the temptation.
>
> As for myself, my business has improved dramatically since I read your book and started using Afformations. Thank you so much!

A client named Tim sent me the following story:

> I'm a consultant for a communications company and had been working with an elderly woman at her house on an issue she had with her home-security system. Every ten minutes, she went outside to have a smoke. After the fourth or fifth time, I asked her if she had ever thought of quitting. She said, "Every day for the last 20 years."

I asked her what she had tried. She said that she'd tried just about everything: the patch, the pill, cold turkey, hypnosis, and many other things she couldn't even remember. It was obvious to me that even though she didn't like smoking, she just couldn't quit.

I asked her if she would be willing to try one more thing. She said she would. I wrote this question on a piece of paper and put it on her refrigerator:

Why is it so easy for me to quit smoking this time?

I asked her to look at it once or twice a day and not to worry about answering it. She said she would.

I planned to check on her again in a couple of weeks, but got so busy that I couldn't get around to it. About five weeks later, however, she had another issue and I needed to go to her house once again.

When I went back, this time I was at her house for over an hour and a half. During all that time, she didn't go outside to smoke—not even once!

As I was leaving, I noticed that her smoking area was all cleaned up and there was no evidence of any cigarettes. I turned and looked at her. She said, and I quote, "I don't know why it was so easy to quit this time."

My response, "Wow, this Afformations stuff really works."

Thanks, Noah!

In my coaching practice and mastermind programs, we don't use the words *good* or *bad* to describe habits. Instead, we use the words *productive* and *unproductive*. Productive habits move us toward what we want, while unproductive habits move us away from what we want.

For example, most people say they want to be happy, healthy, and wealthy. However, habits like procrastination, overeating, and overspending do not move you toward those goals; they move you away from them.

Therefore, when thinking about your own habits, see if they are moving you toward what you say you want or away from it—and adjust accordingly.

> Productive habits move us toward what we want; unproductive habits move us away from what we want.

Remember that The Afformations Method is based on science, not magic. You cannot simply say these new questions, continue to do the same things you've always done, and expect your life to change. If you don't change your actions, you won't change your results.

However, if your disempowering questions are keeping you stuck in habits that are taking you away from what you want, using Afformations can be a great first step to change your thoughts . . . then your words . . . then your actions . . . which can ultimately change your life.

Use the following Afformations to help you overcome procrastination, overeating, overspending, or any other bad habit you'd like to get rid of. Then take new actions, and get ready for the miracles in your life!

Beliefs about Yourself

- Why am I safe to be Who I Really Am?

- Why is it okay to like myself?

- Why is it okay to love myself?

- Why am I so happy being free?

- Why am I in control of my life?

- Why do I easily let go of things that I don't really need?

- Why do I let myself be loved?

- Why do I live my life in harmony?

- Why do I love being healthy and happy?

- Why am I the master of my own emotions?

- Why am I enough?

- Why is it so easy for me to be at peace?

- Why is God right where I am?

- Why am I truly filled with peace?

- Why is it okay for me to be happy and peaceful?

- Why do I give myself permission to enjoy true peace of mind?

- Why did I allow peace of mind to manifest so quickly and easily?

- Why is it okay for me to be incredibly productive?

- Why is it okay for me to have happy, healthy relationships?

- Why can I help more people when I am peaceful and happy?

- Why did I start being a truly relaxed, happy, and confident person?

- Why did God bless me with unprecedented favor today?

Making Better Choices

- Why is it so easy for me to quit _____ (fill in the self-destructive behavior you want to stop doing: procrastinating, overeating, smoking, drinking, doing drugs, overspending, physically or emotionally abusing myself or others, misusing sex, compulsive hoarding, nail biting, and so on)?

- Why was it so easy for me to stop _____?

- Why do I let people support me in stopping _____?

- Why am I free at last?

- Why am I clean and sober?

- Why do I love having a clutter-free home?

- Why did I stop trying to be perfect?

- Why do I feed my body properly?

- Why do I treat my body as the temple it is?

- Why do I have control of my emotions?
- Why do I go to my friends and God for love, instead of turning to something that hurts me?
- Why do I love eating right and exercising?
- Why am I so fulfilled?
- Why do I do what I need to do when it needs to get done?
- Why do I turn to God for my strength?
- Why do I always focus on what I have?
- Why do I always focus on what's good in my life?
- Why did I let go of my need to control everything?
- Why do I live in the present?
- Why do I enjoy relaxing and being at peace?
- Why do I invest my energy in the right things?
- Why do I let myself be as happy as I've always wanted to be?
- Why do I thank God for the peace and joy I have today?
- Why do I choose to be happy today?
- Why am I organized when scheduling my time?
- Why do I love being free?

- Why am I living a life filled with peace and joy?

- Why are all of my decisions so healthy now?

- Why are my actions those of a happy, healthy, and whole person?

- Why do I get to live the life I want?

- Why do I thank God for the abundance in my life today?

• ● •

CHAPTER 15

AFFORMATIONS ON SPIRITUALITY

"I had a million questions to ask God: but when I met Him, they all fled my mind; and it didn't seem to matter."

— CHRISTOPHER MORLEY

Would you like to get closer to God? (It's a trick question.)

I've had many coaching clients and people at my seminars tell me that they want to feel closer to God. I'll often ask them, "Why don't you feel close to God right now?"

They typically answer that they're going through tough times, or that they've just lost someone or something very important to them—for example, a spouse, a parent, a job, or a relationship they weren't ready to let go of.

Then I'll ask them, "Why do you feel that God isn't close to you just because you lost something?"

They reply, "Because God wouldn't take something from someone He loves."

At that point, I usually just look at them, so they can hear what they just said.

Do you know anyone on this Earth who hasn't lost someone or something that was, or still is, very important to him or her?

Loss and *gain* are human ideas, not God's. We humans like to gain, and we don't like to lose . . . but to God, it's all just life. There can be no loss in Spirit.

> There can be no loss in Spirit.

For example, I got this e-mail from Richard, a reader in South Korea:

> Hi Noah,
>
> I was introduced to your book when I was in the U.S. and had to visit the bookstore to read it because I didn't have enough money to purchase a copy. I was getting to know your Afformations and started to use them habitually as I moved to South Korea, where I'm living now.
>
> I started to see and experience little miracles since I began using Afformations. My mind is now programmed with what really I want, and I can tell you this with a smile, because I know that I'm now *in*.
>
> Each event is showing up when I least expect, and I'm getting more and more of the field I create. I realize that I'm the master of my life, not the results.
>
> I feel that everything is connected, and I can see the world differently. There are a lot of positive messages all around, which I didn't see before.

I realize that the world I'd wished for already existed for me, but I didn't see it because I was programmed to receive the opposite of what I wanted. I now can program for what I want easily, since I've been introduced to your book and the Afformations.

Guess what? I now have enough money in my wallet and bank account, and I'm attracting more money for a better future even now. I've got a new girlfriend, who is absolutely one of a kind, and I knew my wish was being realized (before her, I hadn't had a girlfriend for six years).

The thing is that she, the opportunity for my job, and everything else came to me *effortlessly* and *unexpectedly.*

I'm sending and receiving real messages from my new girlfriend even as I'm writing you this e-mail!

She has a very pure, good heart; she's a positive person; and she loves to listen to my stories. I'm sending along a picture so you can see us, too.

Thank you for your Afformations. It transformed my life.

Take care and good luck, Noah. God bless you.

God is all around us. The more I use Afformations, the more I realize that when we feel separate from God, we are the ones who have left. God never leaves us, because God is All That Is.

Use these Afformations (and create your own) to gain a deeper understanding of the fact that to get close to God, you simply need to realize the truth of this couplet:

There is no spot
Where God is not.

Beliefs about God

- Why is God right where I am?

- Why am I One with God?

- Why is God as close as my next breath?

- Why is it okay for me to be, do, and have anything I want?

- Why am I so grateful to be who I am?

- Why does love manifest as my life now?

- Why is happiness Who I Really Am?

- Why is God so happy with me?

- Why is life so fulfilling for me?

- Why am I so enchanting? (A seven-year-old student from Alabama taught me that Afformation!)

- Why do I live by the Golden Rule?

- Why do I choose to be a good steward today?

- Why do I bask in God's Love today?

- Why is my life filled with light and love?

- Why am I connected to God?

- Why does God take perfect care of me?

- Why is my life such a gift?

- Why do I get to enjoy all of God's gifts today?

- Why do I have so many gifts to share with the world?

- Why do miracles happen for me today?

- Why is my life a miracle?

- Why do I have so much to give?

- Why am I always taken care of?

- Why does God provide everything I need?

- Why am I abundantly provided for?

- Why am I right where I should be in life?

- Why has God given me everything I need to succeed?

- Why do I find comfort knowing God is right here for me?

Healthy Spiritual Habits

- Why am I always in the right place at the right time, being the right person and doing the right things?

- Why do I confidently ask for miracles?

- Why do I let miracles happen for me today?

- Why do I give and receive in joyful abundance?

- Why do I have such a strong spiritual center?

- Why do I enjoy true abundance today?
- Why do I ask the right questions to manifest what I really want?
- Why do I thank God for my life?
- Why does my trust in God grow every day?
- Why am I a successful person living a successful life?
- Why do I enjoy the value I bring to others by expressing Who I Really Am?
- Why can I enjoy doing what I want and be a blessing to others at the same time?
- Why do I let myself succeed naturally?
- Why do I happily accept my oneness with God?
- Why do I live each day in God's grace?
- Why do I easily step into my natural success?
- Why do I enjoy the perfect level of success?
- Why do I enjoy showing others the way to natural success?
- Why do I trust myself?
- Why am I worthy of trust?
- Why do I have unstoppable faith?
- Why does my soul rejoice today?
- Why do I have unshakable belief?
- Why is it so easy for me to be and express Who I Really Am?

- Why do I express Who I Really Am by giving myself *permission to succeed?*

- Why do I let my true light shine through in everything I say and do?

- Why do I thank God for the gift of my life, today and every day?

• ● •

CHAPTER 16

AFFORMATIONS ON LIFE AND HAPPINESS

"Don't spend your precious time asking 'Why isn't the world a better place?' It will only be time wasted. The question to ask is, 'How can I make it better?' To that question, there is an answer."

— LEO BUSCAGLIA

Debbye, a client from Texas, sent me the following story:

Dear Noah,

Last Sunday felt like the children's book *Alexander and the Terrible, Horrible, No Good, Very Bad Day!* I had spent all day on Saturday helping cut tons of dead wood out of two trees at my dad's house, so, needless to say, on Sunday I was not only tired but sore!

Late Sunday evening I began looking for my misplaced cell phone. I combed the house, rang the phone, called Dad to see if I'd left it at his house, went through both houses and all laundry, and still no phone.

On the way home from looking all over Dad's yard, I decided to drive by my stepfather's house (which I own) to see if any of his neighbors were having new roofs installed due to damage from our recent hailstorm.

The only evidence of a new roof anywhere on the street was a roofing contractor's sign in my stepfather's yard! I panicked, thinking he had negotiated for a new roof without consulting me first.

Ready for an ulcer, I got home, and still no sign of my phone. My phone service said it was probably lost or destroyed because it was ringing straight to voicemail, so I prepared to file a claim on my cell-phone insurance. They had closed 13 minutes prior, so I couldn't call it in.

As I continued searching for the phone, I then realized I had lost two separate checks, for nearly $10,000 each, that had arrived several days earlier and that I had not yet had time to take care of. I searched the desk, piles of papers, and bank bags, but no checks!

By now I am nearly going crazy!

Ready to drown myself in my hot tub, I called my friend for some "mental garbage removal." Her usual techniques, which normally work, failed this time. Since we'd both read your books, she and I decided to try using Afformations.

We created one for her, and then I decided mine would be, *Why am I so happy?* I jokingly decided that taking a sleeping pill and sleeping until Tuesday, when all the offices would reopen, might be my best option!

Off to bed I went, sarcastically muttering, *Why am I soooo happy?* Just as I turned the corner to my bedroom, what do I see looking right at me from a bookcase? My cell phone!

The battery was dead (hence the no ringing). I had come home from tree trimming, in a very big rush to shower before my dinner guests arrived, and in my hurry had tossed my phone in an unusual place.

Thankfully, because the insurance office was closed when I tried to reach them, I had not been able to file a claim for a new phone.

Early Monday morning (July 4, no less), I decided to call the roofing company on the very long shot that their office would be open at 7:10.

Much to my surprise, someone answered the phone! After a short search, they were able to tell me that the roof in question was not being replaced or even in need of replacement. (Yeah!) The sign had been placed in the yard as advertisement for the roofing man. Whew!

Next, I looked in the tote bag where I keep my bank bags and, lo and behold, there in plain sight was the envelope with the two $10,000 checks!

I couldn't believe how quickly all three biggies were resolved, and on a holiday to boot! Afformations really did the trick!

Thank you, Noah!

As I teach my coaching clients, mastermind students, and seminar audiences, there are two sentences that describe all human emotion. I discovered them while meditating one morning.

Once I saw them in my mind, I realized that these two sentences not only describe our current emotions, but they also reveal how to immediately turn around any negative emotion into a positive.

Ready? Here are the sentences:

When your opinion of your past, present, and future tends to be positive, you will be happy.

When your opinion of your past, present, or future tends to be negative, you will be unhappy.

Those two sentences describe all human emotion. What is the key word in both of those sentences? *Opinion.* Why? Because it's not what happens to us, it's our *opinion* of what happens to us that determines our thoughts, feelings, actions, and responses—and all of those together create our very lives.

Are you carrying around a negative opinion of something that happened to you 10, 20, or 30 years in the *past* and allowing it to determine your life today?

Are you not appreciating all the abundance you have in the *present,* right under your nose?

And are you afraid of what's going to happen to you in the *future?*

If you're holding on to any of these negative opinions—about your past, present, or future—you will tend to be unhappy about that portion of your life. (Many people have a negative opinion about all three!)

Conversely, I'll bet you know individuals who have positive opinions about their past, their present, and their future even though they've been through tremendous pain, unbelievable loss, struggle, and hardship. Let's be honest: how many people do you know who *haven't* gone through these things?

What is it about the people who've been through pain and struggle and choose to be happy anyway? They've made a conscious choice to have a positive opinion about what happened to them in the past, what's happening to them in the present, and what's going to happen to them in the future. They are—whether they know it or not—asking the right questions.

> Your life is nothing more than your opinion of your past, your present, and your future.

There's one more thing I'd like to point out here: *your life is nothing more than your opinion of your past, your present, and your future.*

Where does your past exist? *Only in your mind.*

Where does your present exist? *Only in your mind.*

And where does the future exist? *Only in your mind.*

Nowhere else in the universe do these three things exist than inside that brilliant brain you've been given.

Therefore, if you get nothing else from this book, I really hope you get this—because it's a simple thought that may very well be the greatest gift of this entire teaching:

If you want to live the life of your dreams, change your opinion of your past, your present, and your future.

Right now, I want you to take out your Afformations Journal and write down the opinions you've been holding about your past, your present, and your future. You may be unknowingly asking questions that keep forming a life you *don't* want—because they've kept you focused on what you've lost, what you don't have, and what you think you'll never have.

Well, those are lousy opinions—and the wrong questions.

Guess what? Who is the only person holding them? You.

Who is the only person who can change them? *You.*

And who is the only person who needs to change them, in order for your life to change?

That would be, ah, you.

Now that you're near the end of this book, realize in the depths of your soul that *you* have the power to change your life by changing your questions, and then take new actions that support your new opinions/assumptions/beliefs/questions.

Use these new, empowering Afformations to challenge your assumptions, change your opinions, improve your beliefs, and shift what you focus on . . . and let yourself live the life you've always imagined!

Beliefs about Life and Happiness

- Why am I so happy?
- Why am I more than good enough?
- Why do I attract all good things today?

- Why do I know why I'm here on Earth?

- Why do I know my life purpose?

- Why do I love knowing my life purpose?

- Why am I living my life purpose?

- Why do I know Who I Really Am?

- Why am I so comfortable in my own skin?

- Why did God create the perfect me?

- Why am I so confident being Who I Really Am?

- Why do I attract only good things when I live my life purpose?

- Why do I attract all good things as I express Who I Really Am?

- Why am I perfectly capable of living the life I really want?

- Why am I perfectly capable of living my life purpose?

- Why has God given me the ability to live my life purpose?

- Why am I exactly who I'm supposed to be?

- Why is it okay to like myself?

- Why is it okay to love myself?

- Why am I safe to be Who I Really Am?

- Why do the right people come to me so quickly now?

- Why do opportunities come to me so quickly and easily now?

- Why do highly successful people value and appreciate me?

- Why did God create perfection in Who I Really Am?

- Why am I truly appreciated by my friends, family members, and colleagues?

- Why am I allowed to be Who I Really Am?

- Why do I have more than enough time, money, and energy to do all I want with my life?

- Why am I so lucky?

- Why am I so blessed?

- Why am I so grateful to be me?

Healthy Lifestyle Habits

- Why do I accept Who I Really Am?

- Why do others accept Who I Really Am?

- Why did I stop trying to hide Who I Really Am?

- Why do I only see the best in myself and others?

- Why do I see and accept my own worth and value?

- Why do I accept myself?

- Why does God bless me today?

- Why do I forgive myself?

- Why do I enjoy balance and harmony in my life?

- Why do I easily let go of the past?

- Why do I accept the people in my life just as they are?

- Why is it more important for me to be happy than to be right?

- Why do I leave a legacy of love?

- Why are wonderful people so attracted to me?

- Why do I attract so many Loving Mirrors?

- Why did I stop trying to change people?

- Why am I so grateful for my life?

- Why am I so grateful for all that I am and all that I have today?

- Why am I strong enough to say, "I was wrong"?

- Why do I thank God, every day, for the gifts of my life?

- Why do I explore and discover great new opportunities?

- Why is my life today the best I have ever known?

- Why do I embrace my past, appreciate my present, and step into a better future?

- Why do I immediately take new actions to get the results I want?

- Why do I enjoy living a truly abundant lifestyle?

• ● •

PART IV

NEXT STEPS

CONNECTING THE DOTS (THE REST OF THE STORY)

"You can't connect the dots looking forward; you can only connect them looking backwards. So you have to trust that the dots will somehow connect in your future. You have to trust in something—your gut, destiny, life, karma, whatever. This approach has never let me down, and it has made all the difference in my life."

— STEVE JOBS

There have been a lot of dots.

I was born during the worst snowstorm the state of New Jersey had seen in decades. (Yes, Jon Bon Jovi, Bruce Springsteen, and I all share a Garden State heritage. I'm thinking tribute concert!) Somehow, my parents made it to the hospital in time for my two-weeks-early arrival. My parents have often said that because my older brother, their first child, had been so easy, they assumed that having another would be a piece of cake. Oh boy, were they in for a wake-up call!

Where my brother had been healthy as a horse, I was as sick as a dog. There was one complication after another—I was underweight (needed an incubator), had colic (needed constant care and medication), and malformed legs (needed to wear leg braces like Forrest Gump).

So my parents and I got off to a rocky start. It didn't help that I arrived just as my father decided to leave his cushy advertising job in Manhattan (that paid well) to help launch a summer playhouse in the backwoods of Kennebunkport, Maine (that paid squat).

When I was about 18 months old, my aunt, a school-teacher, noticed that I was sitting on the living-room floor in my grandparents' apartment reading a book. Not just any book, mind you, but *The World Almanac*. In case you're too young to remember, it is an encyclopedia-style book with lots and lots of words, facts and figures, and charts and graphs—real fun stuff for an infant.

My aunt said to my mother, "Do you know that he's reading?"

My mom, a former schoolteacher herself, couldn't believe it—because she didn't have any experience of a child reading at such a young age.

As my school years progressed, I found myself always being "that kid." You know, the one who raises his hand in class because he always knows the answer? (If you're a Harry Potter fan, I'm Hermoine.) Yes, I was that kid the other students would roll their eyes at, because I did my homework and gave the teachers the answers they wanted. "Teacher's pet" was dropped on me more than a few times, along with a few other choice names.

By the time I was about to enter eighth grade, my teachers told my parents, "We don't have anything more to teach him. We think Noah should skip eighth grade and go right into high school." My parents and I decided that I would leave behind the friends I had grown up with since kindergarten and enter high school as a freshman with a brand-new class.

By this time, I had a face full of acne, wore Coke-bottle glasses, and didn't have shoulder-length hair—I had shoulder-*width* hair. (I was a geek, remember?) And it was during this time that I started taking ballet lessons.

Wait, what?! Where did *that* come from?

Oh, right, I forgot to mention that part. Remember when I told you that I had malformed legs and needed leg braces to walk? Because of my condition, one of my doctors recommended to my parents that I start taking dance lessons to strengthen my legs and improve my posture. Around that same time, I saw a movie with Gene Kelly and Fred Astaire where they tap danced magnificently and gracefully. I said to myself, "Wow, I'd love to do that!"

My mom enrolled me in tap-dance classes at a local dance studio. My first dance teacher, a talented man named Jon Miele, took me under his wing and gave me exercises that strengthened my legs, improved my posture, and were also a lot of fun. Plus, I loved all that noise you could make with your tap shoes!

After I'd been taking tap-dance classes for several years, Jon suggested that I start taking ballet lessons. He told me that since ballet is the foundation of dance, it would help me get even stronger. To which I replied, "There's no way you're getting me in tights!"

But Jon kept insisting, and I finally relented. Up until then, I had only ever taken tap classes, which consisted of Jon, me, and two or three other boys. I had never even been in a dance class with (ugh) girls!

That's why, when I walked into my first ballet class at age 15, I was stunned to see 20 pretty girls standing at the ballet barre with their hair pulled back, dressed in leotards and tights. They smiled at me. I smiled back.

Let's see . . . me and 20 girls. *Hmmmm.*

I thought, *Now this is good!*

That's how I came to take ballet lessons throughout high school. After graduating high school and attending college for one year, I decided to leave college to become a professional ballet dancer. This was more of a financial decision than an artistic one. My reasoning was that, as a male dancer, I could get a job at almost any ballet company in the country—because there simply weren't that many of us to choose from. I also realized that I could always go back to college and finish my degree, but a dancer's career has a very short shelf life due to the constant wear and tear on the body. I ended up working for several ballet companies along the East Coast, and was broke and miserable the whole time.

How broke was I? One company, for example, gave me a stipend of $150 a week. This was in the mid-'80s, so it was exactly as little money as it sounds. At the time, I was on the "Pop-Tarts and ginger ale" diet, since that's all I could afford.

How miserable was I? As a professional ballet dancer, the hours are brutal—we worked seven days a week during the season, with classes in the morning, rehearsals during the afternoon, and performances at nights and on weekends—the routine was exhausting, and the punishment you put your body through was essentially willful torture. One of my dance teachers cheerfully described ballet as "a socially acceptable form of the rack." (Yes, she meant the medieval torture device. Pleasant thought, no?)

Why did we—my fellow performers and I—put up with all this? While I can't answer for anyone else, for me it was for one reason only: the chance to perform in front of an audience. When you are flying through the air as if defying gravity, or doing spins that look effortless, there is no feeling like it in the world. It's a feeling that few people on Earth ever get to experience.

But in spite of all my years of sweat, sacrifice, and hard work, I never became a great dancer. I also was very naïve and didn't understand how to play the political games that happen behind the scenes at every ballet company. That's why I often ended up watching in the wings while other guys got all the glory.

A life of dancing is a life of nearly constant physical—not to mention emotional—pain. My comrades and I just accepted it as a fact of life. Sometimes the pain was bad, and other times it was really bad.

Over time, I noticed that the bad pain was becoming really bad; and the pain that had been really bad was becoming excruciating. One night on stage during a performance of *Carmina Burana*—a particularly gorgeous and brutal piece—I was performing a lift when I heard and felt something go *pop* in my hip. That was the end of my dance career.

I was 21 years old. I had no money, no connections, no business experience, and no idea what to do with the rest of my life.

Since I had to find a way to make ends meet, I worked dozens of different survival jobs, and was even more miserable than before. I finally realized that, if I couldn't dance professionally, at least I could act. I decided to move to Hollywood to become a movie star.

I packed everything I owned in my 1977 Buick Riviera and drove from Maine to California with less than $600 in my pocket and stardust dreams in my eyes.

Luckily, a friend from high school who had moved to Los Angeles let me sleep on his couch until I could find my own place. Having no earthly idea how to get a job as an actor, I went to the library and read books on that very subject. They said to polish up your résumé and get a headshot taken. I didn't even know what that meant!

I pounded the pavement going from one audition to another. But Hollywood was underwhelmed by my performance. Every day was a constant stream of rejection: "Thanks, but we've decided to go in another direction." By now I was living in a tiny apartment, barely making enough to survive, and hoping for my big break.

One day in 1991, I was sure it had finally arrived. I auditioned for a traveling musical children's show, and the producer sitting in the audience said he loved how I "took over" the audition. Boom! I went home and waited for the phone call that I was sure would change my fortunes.

A few days later, the phone rang. This was it!

"Hello?" I said.

It was the show's producer. "Thanks, but we've decided to go in another direction."

I hung up the phone and decided I was going to kill myself.

I'm not using a turn of phrase when I say that. When I heard those words of rejection from a total stranger, I decided that I'd had enough of this life. I had been broke since forever; had never known more than a few moments of happiness; and spent most of my life being angry, lonely, and scared. I decided to commit suicide.

Problem: I didn't own a gun. I thought of how I could kill myself without a gun. I remembered hearing how the exhaust from your car engine would kill you if you kept your car running in a closed garage. I decided to do it that way.

Problem: I didn't have a garage, either. In my apartment building, there were only open auto bays, and there was no way to asphyxiate myself in the open air.

I decided to get in my car and drive around the neighborhood until I found an unlocked garage that I could pull my car in, shut the door behind me, and kill myself.

Wouldn't you know it, about 15 minutes later I found myself parked on a strange street in front of a garage with its door wide open. I could drive right in, shut the door behind me, close my eyes . . . and that would be that.

Through all of this, ever since the phone call, I was perfectly calm. I wasn't mad. I wasn't hysterical. I wasn't even upset. I remember the moment I decided to kill myself as a crystalline moment of clarity. It was as if a switch had flipped in my mind: I accepted that I was going to do it, and that was that—as simple a decision as going to the grocery store.

But now, staring at the reality of what I was about to do, I paused. *Think about what you're doing,* someone or something seemed to say to me. *Are you sure you want to do this?*

And then I saw it: the thing that saved my life.

Parked in the corner of the garage was a child's bicycle. It had a white seat and those white things you hold on to at the ends of the handlebars. It looked just like a bike I'd had when I was a kid.

I thought, *Wait a minute. This isn't an abandoned home. A family must live here. What are they going to do when they come home and find my dead body in their garage?*

In my mind's eye, I saw a woman coming home and screaming in shock and terror. I saw a man trying to console the woman, but her being inconsolable, crying hysterically. I saw the bicycle's owner, a child, standing there not understanding what was happening but knowing something was terribly wrong. I saw my horribly selfish act traumatizing this family for the rest of their lives.

And then I saw it: the thing that saved my life.

And I realized that I couldn't do this to them. Even though I didn't know who they were (and will never know), I recognized that what I was about to do wasn't fair to them.

I turned the car around and drove home. That was the last time I ever considered killing myself.

When I got home, I got in the shower—for some reason I wanted to cleanse myself. As I stood there in the shower, I said to no one in particular, "Okay, God, I don't know why you spared me, but you did. I promise to give the rest of my life to you."

I really hadn't talked to God very much before then. But at that moment, it seemed like the right thing to do.

A few months later, a friend told me about a church he was attending and how the minister there was a really good speaker. I had been raised in a church that basically told me that I was a sinner and nothing I did would ever be good enough. (Working as a professional ballet dancer certainly helped to reinforce that belief, since nothing I did was ever good enough!) That's why I was approximately as excited about going back to church as a turkey is about Thanksgiving Day. But for some reason, I decided to give it a try.

I walked into that church, the North Hollywood Church of Religious Science, and heard the minister talk about the nature of God and man. He said, "There is no spot where God is not."

He said, "God and you are one."

He said, "God is right where you are."

I had never heard such things before. I had been raised to believe that God not only didn't like me, but He didn't approve of me and would never be happy with me or what I did. I had never heard of the idea that God could actually be *right here* . . . and actually *like* me!

I started taking classes at the church and learning about the teachings of Dr. Ernest Holmes, the founder of the Church of Religious Science (Science of Mind). I started studying other metaphysical teachers like Catherine Ponder and Deepak Chopra. Then I remembered seeing an author named Louise Hay on the talk show *Donahue* a few years earlier speaking about how your thoughts create your life. At the time, I didn't have a clue what she was talking about. But as I read her books and absorbed her message, I was beginning to understand what she meant.

For the first time in my life, I learned how to pray and began meditating and journaling, learning how to quiet my mind and listen to God. I know that probably sounds awfully woo-woo to some people, but please understand that up until that point in my life, I had been so cut off from my own feelings and opinions that I would just go along with whatever anyone else told me to do. It was the first time I had ever asked myself what I really wanted.

One day, I was praying when I decided to ask God what He wanted me to do with the rest of my life. I'm not sure what I was expecting, but what happened next was the last thing I expected. After I asked the question, I heard a voice say, *Move back to Maine.* The voice came from inside in my head, but the words were as clear as any that had ever been spoken to me.

After I heard the words, *Move back to Maine,* my very next thought was, *Are you kidding me?*

I hadn't lived in New England for nearly a decade, and the thought of moving back seemed crazy. I decided that it was a silly idea and tried to ignore the voice.

But every time I sat down to pray or meditate, the voice would come back: *Move back to Maine.* If my life had been a movie, it would have been *Conversations with God* meets *Field of Dreams.*

The more I tried to ignore the voice, the more I realized that it wasn't going away. As I began to journal about it, it gradually dawned on me that I really didn't want to live in Los Angeles any longer and that my time there had served its purpose. I decided to do something that made absolutely no sense to me.

I sold my car, my furniture, and most of my belongings and moved back to Maine. After working with a business mentor who helped me better understand how I could use my talents and skills, I decided to go back to college to finish my degree. In college for the second time, I decided to major in religious studies and thought I'd end up as a college professor, or even a minister.

And that's how I came to be in that college dorm room on April 24, 1997; experienced The Shower That Changed Everything; and discovered Afformations.

Right after my discovery, I immediately had two thoughts. My first thought was, *Wow, that is so cool!* My second was, *I can't believe no one's thought of this before!*

I then sat down at my Apple computer and wrote the first Afformations: *Why am I enough? Why am I so rich?* and *Why can I do whatever I choose to do?*

These were thoughts I'd never thought before, and the very next thing that popped into my head was: *What am I supposed to do now?* Keep in mind, this was in 1997—years before the advent of blogs and social media; even Google was barely a month old at the time!

I really didn't know what to do with my discovery. Then, on October 20 of that same year, I had the second epiphany that changed my life when I discovered *success anorexia*—a condition that causes people to starve themselves of success and leads to behaviors like self-sabotage and what I describe as *driving down the road of life with one foot on the brake.*

That discovery led to the publication of my first book, *Permission to Succeed*®. Shortly thereafter, people began asking me to coach them and help them get their foot off the brake in their lives, careers, and relationships. I coached many clients through my system, and they started getting amazing results, a few of which you've read about in this book.

I published several other books and crisscrossed the country again, this time doing keynote speeches and leading workshops for Fortune 500 companies and national associations. I had finally discovered what I was here on Earth to do.

But something was still missing. I still didn't have the right systems in my life or my business. I was still trusting the wrong people and not listening to my inner knowing. I found myself in an abusive relationship that ended up costing me tens of thousands of dollars. Eventually, I ended that relationship and closed that chapter of my life, but by that time I was over $40,000 in debt and was forced to move back into my parents' home and work from their basement.

I felt embarrassed, ashamed, and as if I'd let everybody down. But I finally realized that if I had created this life that I *didn't* want, I could also create one that I *did* want. (Gee, isn't it amazing what happens when we apply our own teachings?)

I set about to create a new reality for myself. I started focusing on providing tremendous value to my clients. I learned how to package and promote my products and services to actually turn a profit. (I know!) And most important, every night before I went to bed, I wrote down everything I was grateful for in my life.

At first, my lists started like this: "I'm grateful that I have hands that can feel. I'm grateful that I have eyes that can see. I'm grateful that I have ears that can hear. I'm grateful that my heart is pumping blood throughout my body."

Was this corny? Maybe. But there wasn't anything else to be grateful for—I had no money, had a mountain of debt, and was working out of my parents' basement. What that experience taught me, however, is that we can choose to be grateful, no matter what our outer circumstances are.

Slowly but surely, momentum started to build. Word spread about my work again. More clients started to tell their friends, and those friends became clients themselves.

When money came in, I saved it. Less than six months after moving into my parents' home, I had saved enough to move out and get my own place. Within a year, I had paid off all of my debts and became 100 percent debt free.

Within 24 months, I signed a six-figure book deal with one of the world's largest publishers and became a best-selling author for the first time. I literally went from basement to bestseller in 24 months using this method!

One month after my 40th birthday, I moved to a little town in northeast Ohio. Before I moved there, I'm not sure that I could have pointed to Ohio on a map of the United States. But a friend persuaded me to relocate there, because he lived there and said it would be, and I'm quoting here, "fun." *Okaaaaay.* . . .

A short time later, my friend introduced me to one of his friends, who in turn introduced me to this gorgeous little blonde named Babette. A short time later, I got up the courage to ask her to go ballroom dancing with me, because I figured if I could take her dancing, maybe I'd sweep her off her feet. It turns out that I was the one who got swept off his feet!

Babette and I were married at a perfect ceremony on April 30, 2011—14 years almost to the day after my discovery of Afformations. At our wedding, in front of our family and friends, I gave her this toast: "Because you loved me for who I am, you made me want to be a better man." And I was crying when I said it!

The years since I turned 40 have been the happiest of my life, because in Babette, I finally found my Loving Mirror—the person who sees and believes in me and makes me believe I can do more than I think I can do. Even though I had been writing and teaching people for over ten years about the necessity of having Loving Mirrors, I had never had one myself until she came into my life.

Today our days are filled with friends, family, laughter, and love. I have an amazing team that supports me and our wonderful clients in over 50 countries. I get to lead life-changing seminars and exclusive mastermind groups for people who come from all over the world to attend our programs. My books have now been published in ten languages, and I'm always grateful when I receive a postcard, letter, or social-media post from someone thanking me for something I wrote—whether it's from a person writing in English from North America or in a language I can't even speak from a country halfway around the world!

Are there challenges? Of course; life happens. But they're nothing in comparison to the pain and emptiness of my earlier life. All I have to do is look back and say, "Thank God Almighty that I'm not the person I was."

Every night, I still thank God for the gifts of my life. But instead of thanking Him only for my hands, eyes, ears, and heart, I also thank Him for my gorgeous wife, our beautiful home, my amazing support team, our wonderful friends, our mastermind students, and for our thousands and thousands of fantastic clients around the world. I love you all so very much!

I hope my story inspires you to know that, no matter what challenges you're facing in your life right now, there is a way out—if you allow yourself to let go of the past, step into your best future, and take new actions based on the truth of Who You Really Are.

I would love to help you do that.

• ● •

CHAPTER 18

HOW TO LIVE A MORE ABUNDANT LIFESTYLE IN 28 DAYS OR LESS

*"A good question is never answered.
It is not a bolt to be tightened into place but
a seed to be planted and to bear more seed toward
the hope of greening the landscape of ideas."*

— JOHN ANTHONY CIARDI

This book was written to help you become wildly successful in your life, career, and relationships; be happier, healthier, and wealthier; and create the abundant lifestyle of your dreams. But what do you do now that the book is over?

If you really want the results and benefits you desire for your life, you must do what I shared with you in Part II: *Take Action!*

In Part I, I introduced you to The Afformations Method: the simplest and most effective way I've ever seen to manifest your desires faster, easier, and with far less effort. I showed you how to take something you're already doing—asking questions—and by making a few simple changes, create the life you've always wanted.

In Part II, you learned the Four Steps to create empowering Afformations that can change your life. I urge you to commit to doing these steps daily, because soon you will not only find yourself looking at life very differently, but you will also develop new, healthier habits of living, working, and being.

In Part III, I gave you hundreds of empowering Afformations to help you reach your New Desired Reality in the Ten Major Areas of Life. Of course, if you want to really make changes, and if you want them to be permanent, you must rewire your brain by practicing your new Afformations daily—not just read about it, think about it, or talk about it. . . but actually *do* it!

> Beware of that little voice in your head that will say things like "I can't do it" and "It's too hard."

Beware of that little voice in your head that will say things like, "I can't do it," "It's too hard," and "I don't have time."

As I explain in my seminars and mastermind programs, that's your Negative Reflection talking, telling you that you can't make these positive changes in your life. Remember that your Negative Reflection's job is to keep you right where you are, because its greatest fear is change. Don't listen to it. Follow the formula, and watch your new life take off!

After my discovery in The Shower That Changed Everything, I realized that it was my mission to bring this teaching to the tens of millions of people around the world who desire to live better lives and are also willing to take action and change. That's why my mission is to teach 20 million people how to use Afformations by the year 2020 and assist those who want to live a better life to find their way to true abundance, peace, and joy.

Today, I am truly blessed to lead seminars and exclusive mastermind groups that transform people's lives quickly and permanently. Now that you know how to change your life by using Afformations, I encourage you to make even greater changes by learning my proven formula to dump your head trash—forever—and live a truly abundant lifestyle. And you can do that with my new and improved **Afformations System: 28 Days to a More Abundant Lifestyle.**

The simple fact that you've read this far means you're smart, talented, and highly motivated to succeed. But here's something else I know about you: even though you've already spent a lot of time, money, and effort on traditional "how-to succeed" programs, you're not where you want to be in life. Otherwise, you wouldn't still be reading!

The Afformations System shows you why you're holding yourself back from the success you're perfectly capable of—and gives you the simple, practical tools to create a more abundant lifestyle in the next 28 days or less.

Here's What This Is

The Afformations System is my most popular abundance home-study program. You'll get all the tools, steps, and strategies you need to create a more prosperous lifestyle in 28 days or less, all from the comfort of your home or office.

Who This Is For

This program is for you if . . .

- . . . you're an entrepreneur who wants to rapidly grow your business and leave the struggle behind forever.

- . . . you want to dump your head trash around living a life of true abundance.

- . . . you're a business professional who wants to attract more high-paying clients while staying true to your values and spiritual guidance.

- . . . you want to make more money while enjoying more free time with family and friends.

- . . . you want to stop bad habits like smoking, overeating, overspending, or procrastinating.

- . . . you want to enjoy more vibrant health and attract the happiest relationships of your life.

- . . . you want to learn the same techniques and strategies I've taught my high-paying coaching clients and mastermind students.

What You'll Get

This life-changing program includes . . .

- . . . step-by-step video training and audio guides.

- . . . my complete Afformations Guidebook in a downloadable PDF format.

- . . . access to my private online mastermind where you can meet and network with other Afformers from around the world.

- . . . exclusive interviews with top thought leaders in personal growth and business development.

- . . . my proprietary *Attract More Money iAfform Audio* to change your subconscious thought patterns while you're busy doing other things.

- . . . downloadable recordings of my Elite Coaching Sessions and private Q&A calls with clients from around the world.

- . . . over $500 in special bonus materials . . . *and much more.*

Here's What This Will Do for You

This program will help you . . .

- . . . instantly flip the abundance switch in your brain from negative to positive.

- . . . protect your brain against head-trash intruders and negative programming from outside influences.
- . . . rapidly manifest the abundant lifestyle you've always dreamed of.
- . . . automatically draw your desires to you while you're not even paying attention.
- . . . magnetize money and abundance to you like absolute clockwork.
- . . . command the universe to give you your innermost wishes on complete autopilot.

As a result, you will . . .

- . . . gain bulletproof self-confidence no matter what the situation.
- . . . magnetically attract the abundant lifestyle of your dreams.
- . . . manifest your deepest desires without worry, stress, or anxiety.
- . . . discover how to get more money, more health, more love, more happiness, and more fulfillment in the next 28 days than you've had in the past ten years . . . *and much, much more!*

What Other People Are Saying about This Program

"Since using Noah's program, I tripled my income, renewed my personal relationships, and took my life to the next level of overall wealth . . . all in less than 12 months!"
— **Cari Murphy,** radio host

"Noah, I can't thank you enough for all you have done for me! In less than a month, I have become the person I only dreamed about becoming. I fixed my relationships, my money problems, and my career problems thanks to you."
— **Mladen Milic,** Zurich, Switzerland

"Thank you, Noah, for contributing to my business success. Starting from zero, I skyrocketed my business to over $100,000 in less than four months thanks to your transformational business strategies."
— **Georgina Sweeney,** entrepreneur

"I went from penniless to a six-figure income in six months thanks to Noah's Afformations System."
— **Susan Sherayko,** television producer

Here's What I Want You to Do Now

Go to **www.HavingAbundance.com** and claim your copy of the new and improved edition of my most popular abundance course, The Afformations System.

• ● •

YOUR FREE BONUS GIFT

As a thank-you for purchasing this book, I would like to give you a free *60-Second Stress Buster iAfform Audio.*

iAfform Audios are empowering Afformations set to inspiring music. They help you change your subconscious thought patterns while you're busy doing other things, which will allow you to manifest more abundance and happiness without stress or struggle.

As I've mentioned earlier, you can listen to your *iAfform Audios* anytime, anywhere—while you're eating or exercising, working or playing, in the car, on your laptop, or in your office. Many of my clients even listen to their *iAfform Audios* while they sleep!

You can use them for better, faster results in all areas of your life, including:

- *Ultimate Wealth*
- *Ultimate Business Success*
- *Ultimate Self-Confidence*
- *Ultimate Love*
- *Deep, Blissful Sleep*
- *No More Stress*
- *Live Your Life Purpose*
- . . . and many more

"Noah, I just wanted to drop you a note to tell you that I just signed my first million-dollar deal from a single client. It would not have been possible without applying what you taught me about creating a wealthy mind-set."

— **Robert Smith**, Chicago, Illinois

"Hi, Noah. I got the <u>iAfform Audios</u> on Stress, Love, Confidence, Sleep, Business, Wealth, and Soul Mission. I have now slept without sedation for two weeks. I have fibromyalgia, and insomnia is one of the symptoms. It is a whole new life for me to sleep without aids; I feel less tired during the day and more focused. I am also now starting to feel confident enough to speak publicly to promote my healing practice. Thank you so very much!"

— **Claudette Chartrand**, Ontario, Canada

To claim your free *60-Second iAfform Audio Stress Buster,* please visit: **www.iAfform.com.**

• ● •

JOIN THE AFFORMATIONS REVOLUTION

"The Three Steps to Success: 1) find something that works, 2) tell everyone about it, and 3) repeat."

— NOAH ST. JOHN

Now you know how to create empowering Afformations that can change your life. The only question now is: are you going to share what you've learned or keep it to yourself?

As I've told my clients for years now, the three steps to succeed in life are *learn, do,* and *share.*

First, *learn* what it takes to succeed. That's what this book and my other courses and programs are all about.

Second, *do* the steps. It's one thing to know and quite another thing to put what you know into action. But taking action is the only way to manifest the abundance, wealth, and fulfillment you desire. That's why it's so important to *just do it!*

And finally, *share.* The best way to make Afformations a part of your everyday life is to share your "Aha!" moments from this book through social media, in conversation, and by sharing your Afformations successes with your family and friends.

I encourage you to share with everyone what you've experienced from reading this book and by using Afformations in your own life.

Get the message of this book out to as many people as possible. Commit to telling all of your friends, family members, and work associates about it. Encourage them to purchase copies so they can begin their own life-changing journey. And give your friends copies of this book as a gift that will change their lives.

Consider this: how many times do you run across an idea so simple yet so powerful that it has the potential not just to change your life and other people's lives, but also the world?

Not only will you be introducing your friends to a new way of thinking that will change their lives, but they will also learn a new way of being that will uplift everyone who gets this message.

What better way to make a difference than to show those you care about how to use the greatest gift they've been given—their minds—to make their lives better . . . and ultimately change the world?

Be sure to join the Afformations Revolution and share your Afformation success story at our official Afformations fan page: **www.AfformationNation.com**.

What are you waiting for?

DOWNLOAD THE AFFORMATIONS MOBILE APP

Designed by Noah St. John, the Afformations mobile app is your on-the-go guide to help you change your questions, your brain, and your life—at your fingertips anytime, anywhere!

This app will help you . . .

- . . . instantly remember to use Afformations throughout your day.

- . . . change negative programming into positive thought patterns.

- . . . rapidly increase your ability to attract good things into your life.

- . . . lower stress and increase your self-confidence.

- . . . connect with fellow Afformers around the world.

With the Afformations mobile app, you can . . .

- . . . read empowering Afformations cards at your fingertips.

- . . . e-mail inspiring messages to friends.

- . . . upload photos and videos.

- . . . watch exclusive training videos from Noah St. John.

- . . . get the latest news and updates from Afformations Central—and more!

"Just turn to the life category you want better results in, and you'll find specific Afformations to apply to the situations affecting your life—and instantly start attracting the abundance that's all around you!"

— Noah St. John

Download the Afformations mobile app for Apple and Android devices at iTunes or Google Play.

ACKNOWLEDGMENTS

Special thanks to:

God, the answer to all our questions.

My parents, who sacrificed and gave more than they had.

Louise Hay, for inspiring me at the very beginning of my spiritual journey. I still remember seeing you on the *Donahue* show all those years ago. What an incredible honor that *The Book of Afformations* is now published by the company you founded.

Reid Tracy, for your invaluable advice and supporting my vision to help tens of millions of people live a more abundant lifestyle through the use of Afformations.

My friends, advisors, and colleagues John Assaraf, Jack Canfield, Joe Vitale, Harvey Mackay, the late Stephen R. Covey, Barbara DeAngelis, Neale Donald Walsch, Dr. John Gray, Jay Niblick, Gary Vaynerchuk, Dave Crenshaw, Nick Ortner, Mike Filsaime, Andy Jenkins, Gail Kingsbury, Temple Hayes, Chris Farrell, Anik Singal, Larry Benet, Alex Mandossian, Angie Pohlman, Brendon Burchard, Candace Sandy, Catherine Foster, Chris Baldwin, Chris Byrne, Chris Johnson, Dan Strutzel, Darius Barazandeh,

David Hancock, David Riklan, Denis Teplitski, Dmitriy Kozlov, Denis Waitley, Dr. Fabrizio Mancini, Dr. Len Schwartz, Frank Kern, Gene Grabic, Gillian Ortega, Gina Folk, Graham White, Janet Switzer, Jason Frenn, Jason Holland, Jennifer McLean, Jerry Clark, Jill Banner, Jim Kwik, Joe Sugarman, Joel Osteen, John Counsel, John Harricharan, Jonathan Fields, Joshua Boswell, Joyce Guccione, Julie Morgenstern, Kathleen Deoul, Keith Ferrazzi, Kim George, Kody Bateman, Lance Hood, Lisa Sasevich, Loral Langmeier, Mari Smith, Mary Glorfield, MaryEllen Tribby, Matt Clark, Max Simon, Michael Gebbs, Michael Nitti, Pam Slim, Ray Higdon, Ric Thompson, Rich Schefren, Rick Frishman, Robert Bloom, Robert Hirsch, Rohit Bhargava, Roy H. Williams, Russell Brunson, Ryan Lee, Sarah Shaw, Scott Zimmerman, Seth Godin, Simon Mainwaring, Todd Durkin, Verne Harnish, Will Bowen, and Yanik Silver for everything you've taught me and for your invaluable support.

Arron Alexis, Shannon Baum, Darcy Duval, Patrick Gabrysiak, Gail Gonzales, Shannon Littrell, Lindsay McGinty, Diane Ray, Christy Salinas, Stacey Smith, Heather Tate, Richelle Zizian, and the entire amazing Hay House staff for your endless enthusiasm and devoted efforts to get this book into the hands of Afformers young and old around the world.

Fellow Hay House author Gerry Gavin, whose vision and encouragement helped the book you're holding right now to come into being.

Donna Friedman, Peter Hoppenfeld, and Katherine Reeder for your constant and steadfast dedication.

Damien Zamora, Greg Pelley, Gary Szenderski, Sheila Farragher-Gemma, and the whole GoMobile Solutions

team for helping to develop and launch the Afforma-
tions® mobile app for Apple and Android devices.

Very special thanks to the vast and growing tribe of
Afformers: our phenomenal coaching clients and mastermind students around the world who believe in the
power of this message. Thank you for spreading the word
about our work to all corners of the globe! Every day, as I
hear more and more stories of how the mentorship work
we do together is changing lives, you inspire, encourage,
and uplift me. I am humbled by hearing your amazing
success stories—truly, more than you know. Whether
you're a member of our mastermind family, attend
one of our live or online trainings this year, or simply
commit to telling your friends about this book and the
power of Afformations, I'm grateful for *you*. Every day
brings with it the opportunity to be reborn in the next
greatest vision of ourselves. It's *your* time—let's make it
happen together!

Finally, to Babette: thank you for being the most loving person I've ever met. Thank you for believing in me,
supporting me, and your tireless commitment to help
me put a dent in the universe. I cherish our family and
our three children, and I'm honored to be your husband.

• ● •

ABOUT THE AUTHOR

Noah St. John is famous for invent-
ing Afformations® and creating
high-impact, customized strategies for
fast-growing companies and leading or-
ganizations around the world.

His sought-after advice is known
as the "secret sauce" for creating in-
stant superstar performance in high-growth businesses.

Noah's engaging and down-to-earth speaking style
always gets high marks from audiences. As the leading
authority on how to eliminate limiting beliefs, he deliv-
ers speeches, seminars, and mastermind programs that
have been called "mandatory for anyone who wants to
succeed in business."

He also appears frequently in the news worldwide, in-
cluding CNN, ABC, NBC, CBS, Fox, National Public Radio,
*Parade, Woman's Day, Los Angeles Business Journal, The
Washington Post, Chicago Sun-Times, Selling Power, Bottom
Line Publications,* and *The Huffington Post.*

Noah's books *Permission to Succeed: Unlocking the
Mystery of Success Anorexia* and *The Secret Code of Success:*

7 Hidden Steps to More Wealth and Happiness have been translated into ten languages worldwide.

Founder of the international couching and training corporation **SuccessClinic.com**, Noah is known for his innovative products and programs that have helped to improve tens of thousands of lives and businesses around the world.

Fun Fact: Noah once won an all-expenses-paid trip to Hawaii on the game show *Concentration,* where he missed winning a new car by three seconds. (Note: he had not yet discovered Afformations.)

Noah lives in Northeast Ohio with his lovely wife, Babette.

"Noah St. John's work is about discovering within ourselves what we should have known all along— we are truly powerful beings with unlimited potential."

— **Stephen Covey,** author of
The 7 Habits of Highly Effective People

Get Noah's free video training series: *Discover the Missing Piece to Abundant Health, Wealth and Happiness (All You Need Is 5 Minutes a Day)* at **www.NoahStJohn.com.**

Keep me posted, and keep afforming!

INDEX

Hay House Titles of Related Interest

YOU CAN HEAL YOUR LIFE, the movie,
starring Louise L. Hay & Friends
(available as a 1-DVD program and an expanded 2-DVD set)
Watch the trailer at: **www.LouiseHayMovie.com**

THE SHIFT, the movie,
starring Dr. Wayne W. Dyer
(available as a 1-DVD program and an expanded 2-DVD set)
Watch the trailer at: **www.DyerMovie.com**

• • •

From Stress to Success . . . in Just 31 Days!, by Dr. John F.
Demartini

*The Moses Code: The Most Powerful Manifestation Tool in the
History of the World,* by James F. Twyman

*Truth, Triumph, and Transformation: Sorting out the Fact
from Fiction in Universal Law,* by Sandra Anne Taylor

Wishes Fulfilled: Mastering the Art of Manifesting,
by Dr. Wayne W. Dyer

The Won Thing: The "One" Secret to a Totally Fulfilling Life,
by Peggy McColl

All of the above are available at your local bookstore,
or may be ordered by contacting Hay House (see next page).

• • •

We hope you enjoyed this Hay House book. If you'd like to receive our online catalog featuring additional information on Hay House books and products, or if you'd like to find out more about the Hay Foundation, please contact:

Hay House, Inc., P.O. Box 5100, Carlsbad, CA 92018-5100
(760) 431-7695 or (800) 654-5126
(760) 431-6948 (fax) or (800) 650-5115 (fax)
www.hayhouse.com® • **www.hayfoundation.org**

• • •

Published and distributed in Australia by:
Hay House Australia Pty. Ltd., 18/36 Ralph St.,
Alexandria NSW 2015 • *Phone:* 612-9669-4299
Fax: 612-9669-4144 • www.hayhouse.com.au

Published and distributed in the United Kingdom by:
Hay House UK, Ltd., Astley House, 33 Notting Hill Gate,
London W11 3JQ • *Phone:* 44-20-3675-2450
Fax: 44-20-3675-2451 • www.hayhouse.co.uk

Published and distributed in the Republic of South Africa by:
Hay House SA (Pty), Ltd., P.O. Box 990, Witkoppen 2068
Phone/Fax: 27-11-467-8904 • www.hayhouse.co.za

Published in India by: Hay House Publishers India,
Muskaan Complex, Plot No. 3, B-2, Vasant Kunj,
New Delhi 110 070 • *Phone:* 91-11-4176-1620
Fax: 91-11-4176-1630 • www.hayhouse.co.in

Distributed in Canada by: Raincoast, 9050 Shaughnessy St., Vancouver,
B.C. V6P 6E5 • *Phone:* (604) 323-7100
Fax: (604) 323-2600 • www.raincoast.com

• • •

Take Your Soul on a Vacation

Visit **www.HealYourLife.com®** to regroup,
recharge, and reconnect with your own magnificence.
Featuring blogs, mind-body-spirit news, and
life-changing wisdom from Louise Hay and friends.

Visit **www.HealYourLife.com** today!